In Defense of
Professor Goldrick

In Defense of Professor Goldrick

Colorado's First Schoolteacher and Newspaper Reporter

Margaret McLean Truly

SUMMIT TRAIL BOOKSMITH

Summit Trail Booksmith
P.O. Box 660872, Vestavia Hills, AL 35266
www.professorgoldrick.com

ISBN-13: 978-1-63505-078-3
LCCN: 2016902462

Distributed by Itasca Books

Cover Photograph: Courtesy of Carte de Visite Collection,
Scan #10027713, History Colorado Center, Denver, CO.

Cover Design: Biz Cook

Printed in the United States of America

Dedicated to

James Goldrick
He returned to Ireland, brought his young
brother, Owen Joseph, to America, and
saved the family letters that
made this book possible,
and to
LeRoy R. Hafen
who paved the way to finding the
Goldrick family letters.

*Do not go where the path may lead;
go instead where there is no path and leave a trail.*
RALPH WALDO EMERSON

Contents

Introduction

Colorado's first schoolteacher and newspaper reporter, Professor Owen Joseph Goldrick, was as colorful as the region he adopted as his home. He has been described as eccentric, unique, odd, picturesque, quaint, original, dignified, polite, amiable, erudite, loquacious, a heavy drinker, a lover of children, a ladies' man, and an all-around good fellow. Accounts by people who knew him best indicate these descriptions as accurate.

No one among the Colorado Fifty-niners created more excitement and dismay than Goldrick did on his arrival in the rough pioneer mining town of Auraria (later Denver) on August 10, 1859. He arrived expertly driving the lead ox team of a long train of wagons. Dressed in a silk top hat, broadcloth suit with a cutaway coat, and a neat cravat with matching kid gloves, he bellowed at the oxen in Latin.

Within a few weeks he started Colorado's first school and began writing columns for the *Rocky Mountain News*, a paper that had started a few months prior to his arrival. When pioneers first met him, they were taken aback by his straightforward, clipped manner, but they soon found him to be a quick-witted and knowledgeable charmer. He became one of the most well-known men in the Rocky Mountains and eventually started his own newspaper, the *Rocky Mountain Herald*. He talked and wrote about the events of the day but never about himself, which explains why so little biographical material has been available.

By the time he died, his name was a household word in the area. In a November 27, 1882 obituary in the *Denver Tribune*, a fellow journalist wrote that "while everybody seemed to know him no one knew him well enough to write a true history of his life." His closest associates did not know his full name; he was known only as Professor O. J. Goldrick. What did the "O. J." stand for? Did the widower Goldrick have a family? No one had more than scant knowledge of the brothers said to live in Ohio.

When his friends gathered for his funeral procession, a telegram arrived from a family member asking that the body be sent to Ohio. It was too late. The independent-minded Colorado pioneers decided that the funeral of their fellow Fifty-niner would proceed, and if the family wanted the body, they could have it disinterred and transported to Ohio. Goldrick's body still rests in Denver's historic Riverside Cemetery.

Though the professor has been acknowledged as a strong supporter of the public good, and though a Denver elementary school was named for him in 1952, his legacy is clouded by inaccuracies that have been written about him. Authors have used his writing to bring sparkle and interest to their books without realizing they were using Goldrick's words. The date of birth on his tombstone is incorrect by several years. Early historians Frank Hall and Jerome Smiley gave the year of his death as 1886, even though Hall was one of his pallbearers in 1882. The repeated mention of his heavy drinking by modern authors and journalists has detracted from the fuller story of his role. He is repeatedly said to have died a miserable death in a lonely rented room. Not true.

With so little primary source material available about him, would it be possible to write Goldrick's true story? For several years, I read histories that mentioned him. I followed footnotes and located the sources that authors used and found that these sources were generally the same and contained inaccuracies that continued to be carried forward.

During my research I learned that a breakthrough toward obtaining new information had occurred in the early 1950s. LeRoy R. Hafen, Colorado State Historian at the time, located Goldrick's great-niece, Agnes Goldrick Strothman of St. Augustine, Florida, and procured for the historical society a valuable letter to the professor that had been written by Horace Greeley. Shortly after that, P. M. Goldrick of Indianapolis, Indiana, the professor's great-nephew, sent the historical society two original family letters. One was from the professor's father, written in 1840, and the other from Dr. William O. Goldrick, the professor's older brother.

In 1959, the author of Goldrick's brief and only biography, Nolie Mumey, rendered the professor's first name as Oscar rather than Owen and titled his book *Professor Oscar J. Goldrick and His Denver*. Mumey's biography dedicates only fourteen pages to Goldrick's life. The rest of the slim volume is a reprint of a sketch of Denver's history written by Goldrick.

Robert Perkins, while researching for his 1959 work *The First Hundred Years: An Informal History of Denver and the Rocky Mountain News*, used Hafen's earlier contact and was able to locate another great-niece, Lillian Goldrick Johnson, in North Carolina. She sent Perkins documents that provided fresh information to enrich the few pages about Goldrick that he included in his book.

By the time I began my research, both Perkins and Lillian Goldrick Johnson were deceased. I located Ms. Johnson's daughter, Frances Moody, in North Carolina and learned that she had several old letters relevant to Goldrick. She gave a number of them to me for my research. The letters that had been sent by her mother to Perkins were not among them. Where were they?

I wrote to Perkins's widow. She agreed to allow my research assistant, Gwenth Goldsberry, to go with her to the Perkins family home, which she was cleaning out and preparing to sell. In a shoe box at the bottom of a closet, Gwenth and Ms. Perkins found the missing letters plus correspondence Perkins had had with Lillian Goldrick Johnson. Ms. Perkins graciously gave me the contents of the shoe box to add to my research documents.

Through Frances Moody I located, met, interviewed, and corresponded with six of the professor's great-great-nieces. These cousins were senior citizens and were scattered from California to

Pennsylvania. Each had inherited a clutch of documents, some of which their cousins had not seen. Documents passed down through the generations had become scattered. As I worked with them to obtain information, it became obvious to me, and eventually to them, that the professor's story could never be told until the documents came together in one location. These family members shared precious family letters and documents with me and provided excellent family history. Thus, Hafen's initial outreach culminated in the preservation of many letters and historic documents that had been scattered among members of the Goldrick family.

Goldrick's older brother, William, kept a diary from 1830 to 1886. I was allowed to study the original diary for over a year and to compare it to a meticulously typed transcription that a great-great-niece, Joan Marie Goldrick Johnson, had made. The diary mentions the professor several times and gives insight into the family. When I donated a transcript of the diary and photocopies of some of the letters to the Stephen H. Hart Library in Denver in 1989, Stan Oliner, curator at the time, established the Goldrick Family Collection. In 2015 all of the documents I had collected, plus the ones from Perkins's shoe box, were added to the collection. These include thirty-two original Goldrick family documents and twenty photocopies of additional letters and documents from Goldrick, his brothers, his sister, and his father.

The professor remains a "colorful Colorado character" about whom very little is known. By weaving together material in the diary with correlated dates and information in the letters, and then interspersing citations from nineteenth-century newspapers, I was able to develop a new and more accurate story.

The historic documents written by the Goldricks in the 1800s are now cataloged in archival folders and preserved in the Goldrick Family Collection at the Stephen H. Hart Library and Research Center at the History Colorado Center (formerly the Colorado Historical Society) in Denver. I returned the original diary written by Goldrick's brother, Dr. William O. Goldrick, to the family, and I placed photographs of the diary and the complete typed transcript of it in the collection. Notes on the family's story given to me by Goldrick's great-great-nieces were also placed in the collection. The documents that were saved came from the descendants of Dr. William O. Goldrick, who is buried in Delaware, Ohio. It is my hope that any of his descendants who have documents relative to the professor will add them to this collection so that the material can be properly preserved and made accessible to future generations of the Goldrick family and to historians.

It is fitting that LeRoy Hafen's 1952 outreach to the Goldrick family resulted in the documents used to write this story being preserved in the library of the historical society that welcomed Professor Goldrick as a member in 1881.

Note: Punctuation and grammar were left unchanged in excerpts from diaries, letters, and newspapers.

Chapter I

The Land of Promise

Owen Joseph Goldrick was the youngest and most spoiled child in the Owen Scott Goldrick family of County Sligo, Ireland. In the early and mid-1800s the family lived on a leasehold in the village of Sandfield.[1] The father spoke several languages and was employed by the government as an interpreter. He was a proud man with an independent spirit who boasted that he could talk to persons from elevated walks of life without removing his hat.[2] With a wife, six sons, and a daughter to support, it must have been hard for him when Ireland's economic woes caused his income as a language translator to decline. Fortunately, the land was productive enough so that with the help of strong sons, he could farm his leasehold and provide for his family.[3]

Young Owen, the family favorite, was allowed to forgo much of the manual labor that fell to his older brothers. He managed to absorb some of the language skills of his father, and through the years, he learned enough about agriculture to write intelligently about it much later when he became a journalist.[4]

With six sons seeking to make their way in a country that was suffering, the family patriarch came to accept a hard fact. Emigration to America would become appealing to his oldest sons and eventually to young Owen. The siblings, in order of birth, were James, William, Patrick, Thomas, John, and Ann, followed by baby Owen.[5]

The first to seek the land of promise was William. The second-oldest son, he brooded that he was taking a spot at the family table and doing work that one of his brothers could do. After much anxiety and prayer, he made the decision to emigrate. Fortunately, he was diligent in keeping a diary that would later reveal the family story. Owen was a mere tot when William boarded ship to sail to America. In his diary he describes his voyage and his arrival.[6]

> *June 1, 1831 Blessed be God, after me being 32 days on sea I am no more impaired in my health than when at home. All which the Lord hath done. . . . Glory be to God. I am now near Quebec, the prospect is delightful.*
>
> *June 16, 1831 Lord, have mercy on me. I am this day going to my journey further into the States. Many discourage but I will trust in the Lord with my whole heart and follow the leadings of Providence.*

For the first several months in America, William engaged in manual labor; even in that capacity, he was able to save money. After a time, and with no apparent difficulty, he found work as an educator and became an itinerate teacher, traveling from one small town in Pennsylvania to another as the need arose.[7] Certification of teachers was not required in that state until 1834.[8] William was able to demonstrate that he was both capable and reliable.

In his diary entries, he unfortunately overlooked the opportunity to describe his new surroundings. Preoccupation with the state of his soul and the spiritual state of the people around him indicates that his religion was his rock of salvation—but also a heavy rock to burden his conscience. The following entry reveals his concern for the spiritual life of his family back in Ireland.

> *I have changed my circumstances to another part of the country but the Lord does not leave me nor forsake me. He has brought me among living Christians this day. O my soul, with them to Zion's Hill. I have felt uneasiness enough this week when I reflect on my parents, brothers and sister living without God,*

probably in the world and the fact that I may never see them again. But if the Lord is mine I can give them up to His mercy and be sure that all things will work through Jesus the Lord. Amen.[9]

The family was not living without God, but possibly without William's highly structured version of God.[10] He understandably spent his days in a quest for salvation and inner peace. Theirs had been a strict Catholic family until the father procured a Protestant Bible and began questioning his family's centuries-old religion. His rebellion against the church led to the excommunication of his family. Then he spoke out against what he called "popery." The more vocal he became, the more turmoil the family experienced.[11]

Much of this happened before young Owen was born. William was a brother old enough to be Owen's father and was sensitive to this religious upheaval in the family. Apparently, he enthusiastically embraced Protestantism and over many years, tried one church after another. His brief biography states that he came to embrace the Methodist Episcopal Church and was a devout churchman until his death.[12]

It must have been hard for all of the older siblings to find themselves rejected by friends and family. In a letter to a friend in America in 1834, the father wrote that he dared not be buried in the family graveyard because "I think my blood relatives would think they would serve God by dragging us from our tomb to the river and committing our bodies to the Vasty Deep."[13] In this same letter he said that he had sent William to explore America and that others in the family might follow. He doubted, however, that he would leave Ireland because he had twelve years left on his leasehold, and by the time it was up, he would be sixty-five and too old to emigrate.

During his early years in America, William prayed earnestly for God to help him find a wife. Providence rewarded him. After several unsuccessful courtships, mostly by mail, he met the lovely Matilda Halderman while teaching near Steubenville, Ohio. A lengthy

3

courtship culminated in their marriage. William supported her and the child who would soon follow by teaching. Oftentimes he also traveled as a map salesman. Throughout this time, he dreamed of bettering himself by studying medicine.[14]

Brother James followed William to America in July of 1832 and soon found a teaching job. He was a man who lived his religion by his acts of kindness. James nurtured the family, sent money home to his parents, kept up correspondence with all of his siblings, and saved the family letters for posterity. A lifelong bachelor, he had a fine career as an educator. For a time, he made money mixing and selling various medicines; however, he soon returned to teaching. A frugal and thoughtful man, James always seemed to have money to send to family members in need.[15]

Patrick arrived in America in the fall of 1833. With help from William and James, he managed to support himself with odd jobs. Sadly, within a few years William's diary contains many entries that catalog Patrick's irresponsible behavior and his overuse of alcohol. James, William, and Owen were the three siblings who were blessed with the propensity and ability to better themselves through education. Though Patrick received help and encouragement, he would not commit himself to learning a good trade and eventually took off to Kentucky and other places.[16]

Their father had hoped for a different outcome. He believed that Patrick had the ambition to improve himself beyond manual labor and thought he could become a teacher.[17] That was not to be. On several occasions, William notes in his diary that he and James sent money home and also subsidized Patrick. Both of them undoubtedly had to make personal sacrifices to do so. One letter from Patrick to William thanked him and James for money and then asked for more.[18] Five months later, William's diary entry reads: "My heart is pained about Patrick. O how depraved he is to come drunk about here in my absence. He is inexcusable."[19] William was no doubt mortified that his young wife, Matilda, was left alone to deal with his drunken brother.

Another letter from Patrick arrived. He wrote to William from Circleville, Ohio, complaining that he had not heard from his family and stating that he had no money to visit his brothers. William forwarded the letter to James with a note attached: "James, if you have not yet written to Ireland you can tell them about Patrick, and that he is doing no better than ever. See the consequences of sending him out upon us in this country."[20]

William's life was a struggle. Teaching required that he move about, finding schools that had classes forming up that needed him. The pay was poor for a man with a growing family. Selling maps was more lucrative but required that he travel on horseback away from home for weeks at a time.[21] His dream of becoming a physician required that he save enough to pay for the schooling. In an impressive feat of map selling and frugality, he was able to do this. He took his diary with him to medical school and wrote:

> *I arrived here* [Louisville, Kentucky] *on last evening after a voyage on the Ohio River. . . . The travelling community with some exception are very wicked indeed. Gambling, swearing and immorality. On last evening I heard the first introductory lecture here in the College Hall. It was a nice thing. In God I put my trust in reference to the protection and safety of my dear wife and children.*[22]

William showed great determination. By this time he was thirty-two and Matilda was expecting their third child. James agreed to help finance the beginning of the medical practice with a loan. William wrote to James expressing sincere gratitude. He explained that as a new physician setting up practice, he would not be able to borrow from the bank. The loan from James would make all of his plans possible.[23]

Then, another appeal came from Patrick. He was in jail for drunkenness and theft and wanted money for bail. William made a difficult decision—he would no longer subsidize his brother's

5

dissipation. In his diary he wrote, "His requests to me are unreasonable in extreme. I will let him suffer the penalty of the law."[24]

When William returned home to Pennsylvania from medical college and established his practice, his new endeavor did not thrive. He wrote to James that his Irish heritage was held against him in his practice and that a move was necessary. He subsequently relocated twice in one year, trying to find a place where he was appreciated and accepted. He and his family finally settled in Reynoldsburg, Ohio.[25]

The truth is that William was judgmental of others to a point that caused him to lose support. He was highly critical of people who were not righteous enough. In a diary entry he wrote, "My mind is troubled this evening on account of an expression I uttered in reference to the people here among whom I live 'that they are corrupt.' From this there arose an angry talk on last evening in which I became irritated. The Lord forgive my imprudence and sin. I feel my frailty indeed. It is likely I will be traduced until many of my patrons will leave and I will have to seek a new location."[26]

He held unattainable goals, both for himself and others. If he studied medicine too much, he would then grieve that he was neglecting his religion; but then he expressed in his diary doubts about his abilities and the need for more medical study. He chastised himself for being too outspoken. On one occasion, he noted that a fellow churchman had admonished him about being too critical and sarcastic.[27] Only one person was righteous enough for William and was perfect in his eyes. He never found fault with his wife, Matilda.

William's diary was not all about religion and hardship. By 1847 things were better. The following entry immediately precedes brother Owen's arrival in America. William wrote:

> *When I review my life I am astonished at the goodness of God to me. I was a poor, ragged boy in Ireland. The thought entered my mind to come out and sojourn here in a strange land. Ever since, God has prospered me. I now am a Physician and*

6

have a tolerable good acquaintance with the practice. . . . I am thankful that while my kindred and nation are in so much want I have enough and to spare. . . . I have children but the resources here are great—no one need want who will work.[28]

While William and James were making progress in their new surroundings, their beautiful green isle was approaching a famine in which thousands would die of starvation. Somehow, the family patriarch in Ireland was able to keep his farm going and feed his family.

William wrote to his father suggesting that he send Owen to America and saying, "I don't think Ireland can ever rise from her impoverished condition." He added that Owen could stay with him and his family and pursue a career in medicine or teaching. Their father finally agreed and made a sacrificial decision. He would send his favored son Owen across the ocean. Owen Scott knew that he might never see his young Owen Joseph again.

Chapter 2

The Great Adventure

When Owen was old enough to leave home, James returned to Ireland and fetched him. Owen was an eager youth of eighteen, excited to go on a great adventure—and it soon became apparent that he had more confidence than good sense. James was thirty-eight and had established himself as a teacher in Middletown, Pennsylvania. The vessel *Adario* on which they sailed from Sligo had two cabins. The captain and his wife occupied one. James booked the other cabin for his and his brother's comfort. The remainder of the voyagers sailed in the steerage section. The ship arrived in New York on September 16, 1847.[29]

After they disembarked, James left Owen at 271 Grand Street in New York with a storekeeper and his family. There, young Owen earned board and a small stipend. No documentation is available to explain why James left an inexperienced, callow youth in New York City and took off to Middletown to teach.[30]

For the first time in his life, Owen was on his own. No opportunities existed for him in Ireland. James had literally opened up a whole new world for him. What he would accomplish with this opportunity was up to him.

Ungrateful whelp that he was, he wrote to James to complain about the place where he was staying.

> *I . . . sleep on a cot taken out each night from a back room
> in the very store . . . one of the most disagreeable features of the
> job and trouble, too. The store is pretty cold too, though there
> is a stove in it. Another is that I have to go down under to the
> basement for coal, take it up in quantities each day for the stove
> in the store—have to get wood and chop it and make a fire each
> morning in the stove. . . . The boarding here on the whole is of
> good quality but I may say that the . . . quantity that you can
> have from certain cases is not plentiful. There is rather a good
> table kept.[31]*

How churlish he must have sounded to the benevolent brother
who had brought him from Ireland at considerable expense and found
him a place to stay. He went on to complain about the coffee, saying
that it was the worst, then adding that it was acceptable, but the lady of
the house did not add enough sugar.

As many young people will do, he spoke with authority about the
business of his employer. "He's got 2 or 3 hundred dollars' worth of
goods. . . . The average done (wholesale and retail) each day is from
$15 to $25, one half is easily clear gain."

And then he told James all about New York, even though the city
was not new to his experienced older brother. "This is the greatest
place in the world . . . almost every day some new thing out and about.
. . . Unless I thought I could get easily a situation as a teacher with a
better salary than I have I would rather stay as I am. I have quite a
liking for this business."[32]

When their father back in Ireland heard of Owen's situation, he
was concerned that his overconfident youngest son had been left
alone in New York. He wrote to James, "I prefer Owen being under
your eye. . . . If you visit William you should bring Owen with you.
They are a long time asunder and I am sure Mrs. Goldrick will give
him a warm reception."[33]

Owen wrote to James again from the Grand Street address.

"There are two questions in Thompson's exercises about increase of population. Nos. 9 and 19. They do not follow after simple interest." He went on to say that he had not had time to think much about the problems or to find an answer.[34] Possibly he was using an exercise book that James had provided to help him study for teacher certification. He took teacher certification tests a few months later. It appears that James was helping him prepare to support himself as a pedagogue.

His studies must have progressed well enough to please James because, in the spring of 1848, James invited his young brother to join him in Middletown with the idea of Owen helping him start a select school. James had promotional flyers printed with both of their names listed, advertising the school.[35]

William wrote to them in July of 1848. He knew nothing about Patrick's whereabouts, but he had heard their troubled brother had enlisted in the army. William missed them and suggested that one day they might start up a store near him, with him being the investment partner. He was lonesome for the old country, too. He wrote, "Let us be grateful for the manner in which we were directed to leave a country where poverty and tyranny have blasted the hopes of the most energetic as ever better their conditions. O how I feel when I read of poor starving Ireland. I trust I'll live to see the days when she will be free from bondage in this world."[36]

James and Owen must have had a successful select school for the summer. Then Owen got a teaching job in Intercourse, Pennsylvania, until James lined up an offer for him in Middletown. Showing off his fine penmanship, Owen wrote to James, telling his older brother that he could inform the school board in Middletown that he had accepted their teaching offer. He boasted, "I will subject myself to egotism and say that I am fully prepared to be examined for and teach any of your borough or city schools." Owen went on to say that one of his examiners in a recent teacher certification test had "complimented me very highly on examination day from among the many other applicants there. . . . I felt quite at home in the several subjects of English, literature and common school minutia use." Owen liked the idea of teaching in Middletown because he would be near James "and have a prospect of a good select school next summer if we prove successful and wish to continue there."[37]

Perhaps his living close to James gave the latter cause to complain to William about him. William responded to James, "I think by your letter O. must be a little vain. It is strange then that our family passing through privations and poverty will incline to dress and expenditure of an unnecessary character." Then he added, "Tell Owen to be prudent. He has a great deal to learn and if he thinks not, time will prove his sad error."[38] In his diary William wrote, "I received a letter from James yesterday inquiring about Patrick. He intimated my brother, Owen, to be vain and extravagant. It is singular that our families, raised in poverty, are so inclined to foolishness, but it is so." It is certain that the foolish one he was referring to was his baby brother.[39]

That year, Owen managed to provoke a proliferation of advice from his family, and no doubt needed it. His father wrote to James and included strong words addressed directly to his youngest son. He reminded Owen that James had spent considerable sums of money to help him go forward in life and that if it had not been for James, Owen would likely be working at the Dublin Depot like his friend James Wilson was doing.[40]

He wrote, "I hope you will meet your affairs and not fritter away your time and money in the prime of life as you now are. I hope you won't lay out your earnings on baubles as you were wont to do in Sligo and at home. . . . And above all keep from drink or you will surely perish." He reminded Owen that his brother John, still in Ireland, had a drinking problem, that Patrick drank to his detriment, and that there was a hereditary propensity for dissipation from alcohol on both sides of the family.[41] Owen Scott also mentioned concern for Patrick. "I fear that we will never hear of him dead or alive again." He asked James to check with the war office for any record of his son. He also told James that he had a fine crop and that sending money was not necessary.

"You are very kind to offer money—you have gone too far that way I fear with us all."[42]

Apparently, within a year or so Owen managed to gain his benefactor brother's confidence. James wrote home:

> *Owen is now and will be a successful and popular teacher commanding a high salary. He has improved much in many important respects since his coming out here. . . . He will, if he continues improving in studies thus distinguish himself I think. . . . He has learned some useful, practical lessons since I last wrote. . . . He studies mine and other good books more also and has either no other society, or much better, and from his desire for teachers' associations, periodicals and their acquaintance, he may become an essayist.*[43]

This letter from James must have been reassuring to his father. James relayed that William had repaid all loans and was doing well. "He and his wife are influential and respected in society."

It is apparent that James was proud of Owen because among the documents that he saved is a copy of a teachers' newspaper, the *School Friend*, to which Owen had submitted the correct answer to a mathematics challenge problem. In a letter to James from Dodgeville, Wisconsin, where he had obtained a teaching job, Owen told him that the *School Friend* was a fine journal for teachers. He mentioned other teaching journals and was enthusiastic in listing several books that he thought were excellent. Owen was acquiring a collection of great books and told James that if he wanted copies, Owen had a friend who could get them wholesale. His enthusiasm for learning was high.[44]

All of these happy family correspondences were despoiled tragically when William's beloved Matilda died shortly after the birth of their sixth child. The infant Josephine died as well. Distraught, William had to leave his children with his in-laws 150 miles away while he continued his medical practice in misery and loneliness.[45]

News from Ireland was discouraging. According to their father, John was drinking heavily and was being irresponsible. He was talking of going to America, but his father did not approve and did not want to pay for his emigration. John always seemed to want money from his father. He finally managed to emigrate to the Cape of Good Hope. He found work as a constable five miles north of the Cape and soon had a wife and a growing family. His letters home were sparse.[46]

Within a few months after Matilda's death, the brothers learned that their stalwart father had passed away. He died without knowing what had become of Patrick. James had learned that Patrick's army unit had been disbanded near Cincinnati and that there were many Irishmen working for the railroads there, but efforts to locate the wayward brother failed. The family never heard from him again. They assumed that he was dead.[47]

James and Owen visited William in Reynoldsburg and did what they could to comfort him. Owen then traveled with him to visit his children at the Halderman home in Steubenville.[48] William decided that keeping busy was his best course and returned to medical college in Columbus to get a more advanced degree.[49] The whole family was quite relieved when, a few years after Matilda's death, William married his wife's sister, Clarissa, who had been at her parents' home helping with his children. William and Clarissa returned to Reynoldsburg with the children and within a few years, started a family of their own.[50]

Owen continued to teach in various locations until 1853 when fate took him into a new profession in the publishing business. It is quite possible that his dignified sartorial adornment played a significant role in his acquiring the job. By staying at a fine hotel in Cincinnati, dressed as a successful gentleman, he presented himself at his best to persons who might have employment connections. He did his own form of networking by mingling with the persons in that establishment, letting them know of his qualifications and of his desire for employment. He soon had a job offer as bookkeeper and salesman at Moore, Anderson, Wilstach and Keys, a publishing and book wholesale house in the city.[51]

The job he netted was much to his liking, and he was prepared to give up teaching forever. Though both of his brothers thought him to be extravagant in his dress, they failed to realize that on more than one occasion his personal appearance and demeanor helped him to move forward. The pay was not great, but he was delighted that his employer provided good lodgings.[52] The position allowed him to become acquainted with people of intellect and to have ready access to books of all sorts.

In the mid-1850s the firm published such titles as *Cyclopedia of Modern Travel: A Record of Adventures, Explorations, and Discoveries for the Past Fifty Years* and *History of Medicine from Its Origin to the Nineteenth Century*. With Goldrick's insatiable thirst for knowledge and his love of books, this job surely must have enriched his life. Brother James saved a handwritten sales flyer that Owen, using his fine penmanship, had prepared and sent to potential customers for a book titled *Bartlett's Commercial and Banking Tables*.[53]

Owen stayed in Cincinnati for several years. No documentation is available to tell us when he left the publishing house. In 1857 the country's economy went into a downward spiral. As the 1858 financial depression descended on the nation, jobs of any sort became scarce. News of gold in the Rockies led him to St. Louis, where he hoped to find an opportunity to travel to the West. He was fortunate to be introduced to a wealthy Irish merchant from New Mexico. Owen had never seen that part of the country. Opportunity unfolded before him.

Chapter 3

The Lure of the Mountains

Joseph Doyle owned extensive holdings in New Mexico. A successful merchant, he traded with the Indians, trappers, and miners and provided goods for storekeepers and inns along the way. He hired Owen to go to his large spread to teach his children.

The mode of transport offered to the pedagogue was as a member of an ox-drawn mercantile caravan. After an arduous journey, he arrived at Doyle's compound and began his teaching duties. His knowledge of Spanish was helpful because Doyle's wife was Castilian. Doyle, a generous man, allowed the children of his employees, many of them Mexicans, to be taught along with his children.[54]

After about three months, news of further gold discoveries near Cherry Creek came to Doyle's attention. Knowing there would be another flood of people arriving at the mining settlements, he prepared to send more goods there. His associate, Fred Soloman, had already taken some of the merchandise north to supply the emerging boomtowns. Doyle realized that his adventurous teacher would not be willing to stay at his isolated New Mexico settlement and gave Goldrick leave to accompany the remainder of the large train of goods to the gold diggings.[55]

The arrival of the wagon train on the dusty streets of the small settlement on Cherry Creek has been described by authors as Owen Goldrick's flamboyant, showman-like entrance into the Colorado story. Denver City and Auraria, small competing settlements on either side of Cherry Creek, were composed of shabby log buildings, cabins, and tents. Prospectors from all over the country arrived daily and then headed for the mining areas. Some who brought their families left their wives and children in these crude houses before leaving for the mountain digs. The men remaining in the settlements wore rough clothing and had little concern for their appearance. For the most part, they looked and dressed like the bullwhackers on the wagon train.

Not surprisingly, pioneers were startled and awed when Goldrick appeared, driving the lead wagon and dressed in his formal attire. He must have looked like a dusty version of Abe Lincoln on inauguration day, top hat and all, complete with cravat and leather gloves. Apparently Goldrick stunned the pioneers who saw him expertly handling the ox team.

Since that time, authors have written extravagantly about that entrance. Various ones wrote that Goldrick wore a cutaway coat, a glossy black silk plug hat, striped trousers, lavender gloves, pink gloves, white gloves, yellow gloves, and had a book in his hand, a suitcase containing $500 worth of clothing, a pocket containing fifty cents, a pocket containing a diploma from Columbia College, and a silk waistcoat embroidered with lilies of the valley, rosebuds, and violets. Some claimed to remember the exact words that he spoke in Latin and gleefully translated for their readers what he supposedly said. The story seemed to grow and change with each telling.

In order to explain how Goldrick could be spotless, pristine, and immaculate after driving the wagon over dusty ruts for many days, some spinners of tales declared that he made the wagon team stop outside of town so that he could change clothes.[56] Though families in covered wagons sometimes stopped to freshen up before entering their destination town, even a silver-tongued Irishman might have trouble talking a group of thirsty, tired bullwhackers of freight wagons into stopping so that he could change clothes.

A reliable account could have come from the newspaper. Unfortunately, the town's newly established newspaper did not record

Goldrick's impressive arrival; however, it did note the arrival of the wagon train that brought him to his new home. The weekly *Rocky Mountain News* of August 13, 1859, stated:

> *J. H. [J. B.] Doyle & Co.—On Wednesday evening last, [August 10] the street in front of our office was suddenly blocked . . . the arrival of a large train of large wagons belonging to the above firm, and freighted with over one hundred tons of groceries and dry goods for their wholesale house in this place. For the present their place of business is in the sales room recently occupied by J. F. Wooten & Co.*

An article written years later, with the solid tone of a firsthand observer, appears to have credibility. Excerpted from an unsigned reminiscence piece in the *Rocky Mountain News*, January 1, 1873, the article stated:

> *O. J. Goldrick left the Missouri river with J. B. Doyle's train early in the spring. For some reason soon after starting, the teamsters "struck," and new ones were in demand. Volunteers were called for. The professor rallied to the front in elegant doeskins and broadcloth; immaculate kids; a stunning necktie, and faultless "plug" hat. He took command of the lead team and performed miracles with whip and voice—generally on the off side. The recalcitrant bull-whackers were so charmed with the novel display that they renewed their allegiance to the "wagon boss," and patiently trudged beside their teams all through the summer for sake of the fun. At the old Santa Fe crossing of the Arkansas the train divided, half going to Fort Barclay, New Mexico, where Mr. Doyle had an extensive establishment, and the other half heading for Pike's Peak. Fred mounted his mule and beat his train to Cherry creek by ten days. Goldrick went to New Mexico and three months later made his debut on Ferry Street with the other half of the original train. Wristlets of kids*

encircled his hands; his "stove pipe" was weather-beaten, rusty and napless; his doe-skin pants glossy and slick; his broadcloth coat darned and seedy; but all were as faultlessly adjusted as they will be to-day in his rounds of New Year's calls. He was the Beau Brummel of the camp, and the first specimen of a gentleman in full dress ever seen in these diggings.[57]

Was Owen Goldrick attempting to make a spectacular entrance into the ragged little town, or was he dressed in a dusty version of the attire he had always worn since the early days when he earned his first paycheck teaching and listened to his brothers' complaints about his extravagant sartorial tastes? What can be guaranteed is that after he cleaned the dust off of his person, he presented himself immaculately dressed, and was never seen dressed any other way, from that time on.

Several of the accounts mention his bringing with him a suitcase containing $500 worth of clothes and having fifty cents in his pocket, which he promptly spent on a cigar and a shot of Taos Lightning. These stories are probably true. No fine clothes were available to purchase at Cherry Creek at that time. Goldrick must have brought a supply with him to keep himself elegantly turned out. The story about the fifty cents was told by Goldrick to his colleague, W. B. Vickers, who relayed it to the readers of his 1880 *History of Denver.* Vickers went on to say that shortly after his arrival, Goldrick "walked up the street with an air so lordly that people looked at him as though he had just bought the town, and would take possession as soon as the papers were made out."[58] The pioneers were impressed with his confidence and his winsome sense of humor.

Goldrick's longtime habit of dressing for success may have once again drawn attention to him and helped him to secure employment. The pioneers were immediately interested in him and his potential. Many have written that as soon as he arrived, he began to pass his top hat for money for a school. That was untrue, and it was not necessary.

The people swept him up, named him "Professor," and two civic-minded fellows began a subscription drive, going about town collecting pledges to start the school.[59] Goldrick supported and encouraged this effort. He needed employment and enjoyed being sought so quickly for the job. Also, no doubt he could not imagine a town with children but no school.

The two civic-minded men, a Mr. McAfee and a Mr. Ross, were enthusiastic gentlemen who knew the value of education and how a school would encourage community development. A few days after Goldrick's arrival, a letter from Mr. McAfee expressing strong support for a school was published in the weekly paper.[60]

No one gave more support to the effort than W. N. Byers, the co-owner-editor of the *News*. Though only a few months old, this newspaper strongly supported civic improvements in the area. Byers drew attention to McAfee's letter, saying, "The prospects are bright and there can never be a more fitting time than the present to commence the improvements suggested by 'H. H. M.' in his excellent commentary."[61]

Things moved quickly after that. On September 22 the *News* noted:

A movement has been set on foot by the citizens of Auraria and Denver to raise means to erect a union school house for the use of both towns the coming winter, and we learn from Mr. Ross, who has been circulating the subscription paper, that about two hundred and fifty dollars are already subscribed and he thinks there is no doubt but that a sufficient amount can be obtained to build a comfortable house for school purposes this fall. Those wishing to contribute to this enterprise will find the subscription paper in the hands of Mr. Ross.

The pressure was now on to open the school. When it became evident that funds would not be sufficient to build right away, the school was opened in a rented building. Professor Goldrick's card announcing the school appeared in the September 29 *News* a few weeks after his arrival. The *News* stated, "Please notice Card of Prof. Goldrick's School in another column."

UNION DAY SCHOOL The subscriber would respectfully announce to the citizens of Auraria and Denver City that the above School will be opened on Monday, October 3, in the room lately occupied by Col. Inslee, Auraria, until a more commodious and comfortable school room and school furniture is made ready.

From many years experience as Principal and Superintendent of Schools and Academies in the East, and familiarity with the latest approved modes of teaching and successful governing he trusts to be able to secure the speedy and substantial improvement of all grades of pupils that may be committed to his care, and to build up a first class school, wherein the young will be thoroughly grounded in the elementary and practical studies, and the more advanced prepared for college or the counting room.

Pupils may enter by the month, and continue while convenient, as each scholar shall receive a due share of individual attention, adapted to his or her peculiar wants and capacity. For particulars, inquire at the school room, or refer to R. L. Wooton, Esq., Auraria and Joseph Richard, Esq., Denver City. Terms moderate. O. Goldrick, Principal.

Chapter 4

Pedagogue — Journalist

The school was located on the Auraria side of Cherry Creek, so it was named the Union Day School to indicate that it was for both sides of the creek. Intense rivalry that existed between Auraria and Denver City was not ameliorated by the name. Every time a prairie schooner with children aboard rolled into either settlement, the folks in Auraria shouted for them to settle in their town where a school already existed.[62]

The description of the school was well documented by Goldrick in an article he wrote years later:

> *The first school was founded in Denver, or in Colorado . . . was opened on the third of October, 1859, by the present writer, in a small log cabin near the corner of Twelfth and Blake Street, West Denver. The hut had a flat roof which was a great conductor of snow and rain, much to the discomfort of the dear little urchins during wet weather. A small gable at the end sufficient for an unglazed window, and a strip of wagon cover hung down to the ground, covering the hole that the log carpenter left for a door until some sawmill should supply dressed lumber.[63]*

The professor's first months in the mining communities were busy and exciting. By his fourth month in residence, he was not only teaching but also moonlighting as a freelance reporter for Byers at the *Rocky Mountain News* and writing an anonymous column for the *Missouri Democrat* using the pen name Observer.[64]

One of his first articles for the *News* was a piece about Zebulon Pike and his discoveries in the region. After telling the story, Goldrick pointed out that an explorer of Pike's caliber needed a solid education. The professor ended on a note that expressed the importance of study and learning. He wrote that with all great civilizations, a great effort to improve the mind is of paramount importance.

> *School instruction does not call genius into existence, but at the same time, without it, genius will remain chained in the mind, useless and unimproved. Smelting does not make the silver, but without smelting it would never be anything but ore.*[65]

Goldrick had a retentive mind and insatiable curiosity. Thus, he was able to tuck away information and use it later when writing his articles. Writing from memory, he described the New Mexico farmers' homemade implements, such as a crude plow made solely from wood.

> *A section of the trunk of a tree, eight or ten inches in diameter, is cut about two feet long, with a small branch left projecting upwards of a convenient length for a handle. With this a beam is connected to which oxen are yoked. The block, with its fore end sloped downward to a point, runs flat and opens a furrow similar to that of a common shovel-plow. What is equally worthy of remark is that these plows are often made exclusively of wood, without a single particle of iron, or even a nail, to increase their durability.*[66]

His contributions to the *News* were wide ranging in their subject matter and helped fill the pages of the paper that was too isolated to tap normal news sources. His anonymous Observer letters to the *Democrat* were so sensational that people fought over copies when the stagecoach from St. Louis arrived with the week-old copies containing his articles.

The *News* stated:

> *We hereby request the publishers of the* Missouri Democrat
> *to print our copy on linen, or send a great number of copies to this*
> *country, or else quit publishing the letters of the "Observer." The*
> *paper is too attractive; for three successive numbers preceding*
> *the last, we did not get to read it at all. The last one we loaned*
> *seven times, to persons who—as near as we can learn—each*
> *loaned it eleven times; consequence, when our turn came to read*
> *it, it was in sixteen pieces with numerous rents, dog ears, and*
> *obliterations to each."*[67]

In a reminiscence piece long after Goldrick's death, A. E. Pierce,
who established the first newsstand, wrote:

> *The St. Louis* Democrat *and the* Republican *were the*
> *most popular papers, especially the* Democrat *for which the*
> *immortal O. J. Goldrick was the "Pike's Peak Correspondent,"*
> *and his regular and racy letters under the nom-de-plum* [sic]
> *of "Observer" attracted wide attention. So many copies of this*
> *paper were sold here that a special edition with my name across*
> *the top was printed, and the same distinction was accorded my*
> *competitors, Woolworth & Moffat.*[68]

Goldrick was often the first person to meet the stagecoach arriving
from St. Louis, so that he could get information for the *News*,[69] and
when the coach left to return to St. Louis, it would carry his letter to the
Democrat signed "Observer." Thus, he was able to draw some income
from both papers, plus the small stipends from his school students.

Some readers accused the Observer of exaggeration and boosterism
of the area. Writing under his pen name, Goldrick told his readers that
this was the greatest gold find ever, but he also cautioned them repeatedly that all who came would not get rich, and that mining required planning, provisions, perseverance, and extremely hard work and sacrifice.[70]
He believed what he was writing. This is evidenced by the fact that he
sent his brothers the same encouraging advice that he gave his readers.

He advised his brother James "definitely and conclusively to come immediately . . . per express coach from Leavenworth City."[71] In another letter to James, he wrote:

> *I write this to you that there is the greatest opening to make a few hundred dollars invested judiciously in valuable city lots which . . . will command two to four times that amount by the first of July next when hundreds of thousands of capitalists and merchants will arrive here to buy and build stores.*[72]

Writing as the Observer, he had the same advice for single men:

> *The quickest and cheapest route for single men is Leavenworth express coaches. . . . A capitalist coming out here by express the next few weeks, with the "spondulicks," could make ten thousand out of two or three by the first of July next.*[73]

For his married bother, William, who was then living and practicing medicine in Marysville, Ohio, he wrote different advice. It was the same advice that he wrote in the *Democrat* to men with families:[74]

> *Now Doct* [sic] *if you are making money, I will not press you to come out here—but if you are not doing well, I want you and all the folks, to make up your mind to prepare. . . . I believe this to be the great place for this Union—and by you all coming out here in time, and roughing it in the bush, at one thing and another—we all can be both profitably and prominently enriched before four years to come.*[75]

William may have taken a trip to Cherry Creek to check out the scene. An arrival by stage of a William Goldrick was recorded with no date, and Dr. William Goldrick's name appears in the *Auraria Land Record* dated March 1860.[76] William's notes in his diary for this period are missing, and no letters illuminate these records.

It is doubtful that James was interested in buying lots at that time. He had problems to solve an ocean away. His brother Thomas wrote from

Sandfield regarding trouble in the family. Ann was trying to manage her farm alone after the loss of her husband, and according to Thomas, had mismanaged so badly that she was in danger of losing it. She sold all her hay and then had no feed for her cattle. Thomas had to sell a cow and loan her money. John was working near the Cape of Good Hope. He had a wife and several children to support, and had always been more of a burden to the family than a help. To add further pressure to James, Thomas reported that their ailing mother said that she would surely die if Ann and the children came to live with her and Thomas.[77]

During this time, Owen was involved in his new community. In his teenage years in Middletown, Pennsylvania, he had participated in a Sunday school. It had been a growing and successful concern that gave the youth a wholesome environment in which to meet and study the scripture.[78] Therefore, when a dignified gentleman named Lewis N. Tappan walked past the school in Auraria, saw the children congregated, and suggested that a Sunday school would be good for the community, the professor readily agreed. The two men immediately called a committee of prominent citizens together to formulate plans. One month after the school had opened, the interdenominational Union Sunday School began. The effort thrived until various denominations established themselves and commenced their own Sunday schools.[79]

Another positive endeavor was the Library Association and its reading room. The professor worked on this project with his friend Arthur E. Pierce. They had ninety-nine initial subscribers. The original minutes still exist showing the list of members. Beside the name of John Shear, Pierce could not resist writing, "Lynched and hung August 1860 for horse stealing." Such were the times in which they lived. The board of the library charged a small monthly fee to cover purchase of periodicals and books.[80] The enterprise was successful for several months. In a reminiscence piece, Pierce told why it dissolved:

> *When the echo of the guns firing upon Fort Sumpter*
> [sic] *were heard, there was a general breaking up of Denver*

and Colorado society. There were many Southerners here and partisan spirit ran high. This writer and many others left for their Northern homes and joined the Union Army. Many others left for the South and united with the Confederate forces.[81]

Goldrick made no claim that he spent all of his time in worthy pursuits. The twin mining towns were rough settlements, and though many of the outstanding, upright citizens were part of Goldrick's life, others, baser in their leanings, preferred to spend their time drinking, gambling, and telling tales about the mines. Though the professor avoided gambling, he visited the saloons often. There, he got the latest news from the diggings. Also, he was a drinking man who enjoyed, but complained about, the watered-down whiskey.

Potential emigrants who read Goldrick's Observer columns had no need for a guidebook. He examined every potential route and gave suggestions for each, telling the folks what they might encounter and pointing out commercial spots where they could purchase additional supplies along the way. The list of supplies that he recommended to families was exhaustive.[82]

Further, he pretended as the Observer to interview Principal Goldrick of the Union School. This provided an opportunity for the schoolmaster (himself) to list four paragraphs of books that pioneers should bring for their school-age children. He provided detailed lists of supplies the schoolchildren would need. To this, he added recommendations of entertaining, informative books for adults to read while on the trail. Among them were biographies of Kit Carson and Jim Beckwourth—books that would set the mood for their adventure.[83]

Goldrick's obsession with books is revealed in his Observer columns. He advised potential emigrants to bring their Bibles, as there were some towns that did not even "have a Bible to swear upon."

Be sure and bring along your best books, not forgetting your full library of standard works, if you are a lawyer, doctor, or other professional man. Do not come without a great bible and hymn book of your persuasion, also a family bible, if you have one, not forgetting a copy of Webster's Unabridged Dictionary, *grand new edition with illustrations. . . . These libraries, if they are great for anything, will be worth a great deal . . . here, if you ever wanted to sell them, than you may imagine.*"[84]

The long list of recommended schoolbooks and other books for families to bring suggests that there would be scant room left in the wagon for all of Goldrick's other suggested items, much less room for the children.

Goldrick allowed his Observer readers to share the ebullience of the pioneers:

The tide of mi-o-neers is rolling in upon us at the rate of a hundred a day, and full as many are rolling out for the various sections of the mountain mines. All now is life, bustle, travel and rush, hopes and expectations. You insult a man here by offering him a big figure for daily labor; he is preparing to go to the mountains to be his own boss, and expecting soon to be his own banker.[85]

Some of the pioneers were coming through southern Colorado, so he described the route north through the Colorado City area. His letters to the *Democrat* were read extensively back East and may have contributed to the idea of many to visit the healing springs that eventually turned the area into a famous health spa. He wrote:

Indians, chiefs, squaws and papooses betook themselves here and from time to time immemorial, and found immediate relief and health restored. Fome [sic] of the waters, put once or twice on the sores of horses and the sore backs of mules, and Mexican jacks, do at once clear up the same. The waters are at once exceedingly exhilarating and exceedingly and peculiarly pleasant—you can drink a quart almost at a time, and feel afterwards and all that day as if you could jump as high as an

Indian rubber ball, and vigorous enough to hold a fist fight with a grizzly.[86]

The flow of words from the pedagogue's pen created a permanent record of Goldrick's view of milestones in early Colorado history. His Observer paragraphs were peopled with such characters as George Russell, William Byers, Kit Carson, Jim Beckwourth, Samuel Hawkins, and Mountain Charlie. He capably recorded events such as the arrival of the first wind wagon on the streets of Denver, and the goings-on in the Union Sunday School, the Union School, the Episcopal Church, and the Library Association, all of which he helped to establish. His Observer reports to the *Democrat* gave people back East vivid images of what was happening in the gold country.

One event, a turning point in Colorado history, took place in the moonlight on the night when Denver City and Auraria officially merged. The ceremony appropriately took place on a bridge that joined the two towns. Goldrick's Observer account of this event appeared in the April 21, 1860, issue of the *Democrat*.

> *Gen. Wm. Larimer referred to our earlier history and suffering here during the pioneer years of '58 and '59, stating that when he and party first crossed this Creek at the very spot over which we now stood on their fine new bridge, some eighteen months ago, all here then was supposition and doubt, in the midst of a houseless handful of hardy pioneers . . . here we are destined to have the rich capital of another strong and loyal State, with population before long of thirty to fifty thousand, and a state or Territorial population of several hundred thousand and before many seasons hence, when we shall inevitably be another San Francisco as far as business and gold yields are concerned.*

Larimer's speech was an optimistic one that suited the occasion. The reality was that the dusty, crude, lawless little towns, even when combined for strength, had much work ahead to make these words blossom into truth.

Though the new Denver was scruffy and struggling, it had some refinements. The professor was a leader in the Library Association, and enjoyed having the Observer tell the people back East about the town's intellectual pursuits. He reported on the formation of the association and its purposes, describing the lecture at the third meeting. Mayor John Moore's talk entitled "The Influence of Literature upon Civilization" was well received. A large audience filled the rough benches in Apollo Hall. Goldrick remembered the ladies, adding, "There were more good-looking and intelligent lady hearers out on this occasion than on previous occasions, and all went off in the most satisfactory and acceptable manner."[87]

The addition of prodding humor to his column was typical of the professor's writing. He made his point and softened it with humor as he challenged the pioneers on their impropriety in dealing with the Indians.

> *Getting up outfits of wagons and mules, or oxen, and going up to trade with the Sioux, is getting to be one of our everyday occurrences here in Denver City this winter season. If you push me to the wall to tell, I must state in the language of Demosthenes about action in oratory, slightly altered, that the first chief staple for the trip is whiskey—the second chief staple is whiskey, and the third and last is—whiskey. However, sugar, coffee, and tobacco are thrown in, of course, by the way of adding appearance of variety to the outfit.*[88]

Along with his fun-loving accounts of goings-on at the theater, and the pining of young men pursuing the scant number of lovely young ladies, he also wrote about serious matters. The establishment of the Episcopal Church in the town caught his imagination. He readily offered them a meeting place in his schoolroom until they could find a more suitable spot. Perhaps he was thinking of his benevolent older brother James, a devout Episcopalian, when he wrote the following in an Observer column.[89]

> *I know not how or why, or wherefore, but it has always appeared to me that where you find a community or city that embraces among its citizens a goodly number of gentlemen and ladies of the Protestant Episcopal persuasion that the society there is all right—intelligent and agreeable—as a first class community to live amongst.*[90]

The pioneers had just celebrated the Christmas season when he wrote a sentimental segment as the Observer about young men coming to the mountains with high hopes. He had done just that and had been at Cherry Creek about five months when he wrote:

> *Another thought has often lately suggested itself to me, here, how many city bred young men, who all their lives were handled tenderly and raised pets, in a fit of irrepressible ambition for sudden wealth, have been traveling today after their claims or their cattle, on these Rocky Mountain ridges, have crawled over 700 miles of sameness and severity across the dreary plains, have settled and sobered themselves down in noiseless canyons or river bottom ranches, putting in the same existence which a year ago they disposed of and displayed in an entirely opposite and different style in the States. But, so it is, and such is life—the far off prospect always seems most fair, and we are glad that in this section it has proved to be so in reality.*[91]

Though Goldrick had not become wealthy from the mines, he had been well received by the people. He was teaching school and writing—the same things he had done back in the East—but the prospects "turned out fair" in his Rocky Mountains.

He let the readers back East know that there was an active social life in Denver, with many amenities. A description of a wedding feast demonstrated that the wild game, fruits, and berries in the region, along with imaginative cooks, kept the pioneers eager for parties and celebrations. He told about stringed instruments playing in the home of Col. J. D. Henderson, fifteen miles north of Denver. His description makes the reader want to tap his toe:

> *Pretty, pleasant women and gallant gentlemanly men reveled in enjoyment, and rivaled each other in deeds and dignity. White kids and light kids, satin slippers and patent leathers, shone and stepped around with commendable celerity, while the more antique, the white, pink, blue and orange colored satins rustled all through as vauntingly and voluminously as good-looking women now-a-days generally do. For interest, pleasure, fashion, and handsome enjoyment, the affair could not be outdone in your city anywhere.*

Mrs. Henderson served the following: decorated prairie chicken salad, braised wild turkey, aspic of oysters, decorated aspic of antelope brains, black-tailed deer cutlets, buffalo tongue, broiled chicken, ham in champagne sauce, deer and antelope ribs, bear meat with Madeira sauce, hot slaw, apple pie, cream meringue, and coffee, as well as sweet breads, jellies (made from wild strawberries, raspberries, and currants), macaroons, pecans, almond puffs, almond filberts, and lady fingers.[92]

Colorado's mining district encompassed a region of great contrast. The Observer did not spare his readers the true stories of the murders, hangings, duels, and gunfights that occurred almost weekly. Nor did he forget to mention the dozen people killed by Kiowa Indians 150 miles from Denver as the victims attempted to find another route to the mines.[93]

Goldrick discovered a strange conflict within himself. Though he encouraged emigration, which sometimes filled the streets with covered wagons as far as one could see, he also felt sympathy for the Indians. The more peaceable ones would stand with quiet dignity outside the church doors, peeking in with perplexed faces as they saw the ritual and heard pioneer church songs. Goldrick had demanded in print that the territorial government protect the pioneers from hostile Indians, but he also wrote:

> *Poor honest Indians! I don't know what they'll do or where they'll go in a few years more. American progress here usurped the hunting grounds! Their arrows are broken, and their war cry is hushed! Their campfires have gone out, and the places where they were wont to locate their lodges now know them no more! They come and look, and talk to each other in amazement about the signs and intrusions of civilization in this city here. They cast a last glance at the junction of the Platte and Cherry Creek— the favorite village grounds. They see coaches and carriages driving over their trails. . . . They shed no tears, but they sigh with wonder! For here, where . . . the buffalo wandered, and the wild deer loved to roam, they now can neither trace the one nor catch the trail of the other.[94]*

The pioneers were living in times that were exciting and promising and yet, filled with danger. Journalist Albert Richardson recorded a good description of their environs:

> *Denver Society was a strange medley. There were Americans from every quarter of the Union. Mexicans, Indians, half-breeds, trappers, speculators, gamblers, desperadoes, broken-down politicians and honest men. Almost every day was enlivened by a little shooting match.[95]*

This was the nature of the place, and Goldrick's eagerness to write clever, spectacular pieces for the *Missouri Democrat*, while posing as the Observer, got him into serious trouble that almost cost him his life. Historians refer to this episode as the McClure-Goldrick incident. Goldrick considered it his close brush with death.

Chapter 5

A Brush with Death

At first it was safe for the professor to write what he wished for the *Democrat*. He was hiding behind his *nom de plume*. Some of the things he wrote were controversial, but that is what made the newspapers sell so well. He enjoyed tantalizing his readers, daring them to guess the identity of the Observer.

> *The great query, during the past week, in Denver and Auraria, was, "who writes for the* Missouri Democrat*?" . . . As high as one hundred dollars . . . was offered around the saloons for the person of your humble servant . . . but, thanks his stars, he was not identified.*[96]

Pioneers were willing to pay two dollars for week-old copies of the *Democrat*. Considering that the local papers sold for twenty-five cents, this was a grand price.

Goldrick enjoyed leaving clues to baffle the readers and once wrote, "Indeed, there is not a second man or firm in this city who knows me in this, my capacity of correspondent."[97] He sometimes injected statements to deliberately mislead his readers. The Observer stated that he had arrived in May, when it was well known that the professor had arrived in August. In another piece, he mentioned that he had not been able to attend a fine party because he, the Observer, was panning for gold. When he mentioned the schoolteacher, he pretended that he did not know how to spell the name, and wrote, "G—" to indicate the name.[98]

35

Some of the sentiments that he expressed as the Observer were quite partisan. During those times, sectional loyalties were high. He surely stepped on some toes when the Observer commented about the arrival of a party of Georgians who traveled "with two colored servants, probably contented slaves, if there be such. I don't know exactly how such things may work here in the mines at present, but I rejoice to believe that in a year or so more, when we have a free gold, liberty-loving State or Territorial majority, the curse of active slavery should not be allowed to blacken our golden banners."[99]

At times, he was careless about hiding his identity. He was writing freelance articles for the *Rocky Mountain News* and occasionally wrote something identical when writing as the Observer. What saved him for a time was that it took at least two to three weeks for his letter to leave Denver/Auraria for St. Louis, be printed in the *Democrat*, then return in that paper to Cherry Creek. By then the readers had forgotten the exact words Goldrick had used in earlier copies of the *News*.

A careful reader of both papers would have no trouble identifying instances of his carelessness. For example, it was generally known that Goldrick was fluent in Spanish. A conspicuous clue was that he frequently used Spanish phrases while writing for the *News* and as the Observer for the *Democrat*.

When describing the mountains to the south, he wrote in the *News* about "the 'yellow banks of Pike's Peak,' as eastern journalists would say." On the same day, as the Observer for the *Democrat*, he mentioned "the 'yellow banks of Pike's Peak,' (as eastern journalists would say)."[100]

Another example is the John Greenleaf Whittier poem that he altered slightly in the *News* and also as the Observer. The last line should read, "its muscle and its mind!" He changed it in both papers to read, "its muscle and its mines."[101]

A clue that would be hard to ignore is that he traveled to the mines for the *Rocky Mountain News* in July and August. During that time, he wrote articles for that paper signed "G." In that same time frame, the

Observer skipped a few weeks, and then resumed his column, stating that he had been traveling in the mountains looking at the mines.[102] Again, the only thing that preserved his identity was that people read the Observer articles two or three weeks after they read his material in the *News*.

Park McClure was the local postmaster. He was a strong supporter of the South seceding and forming its own government. Goldrick made no attempt to hide the fact that he was in favor of preserving the Union. He expressed this opinion openly in the mining community and did not hide behind the Observer. Also, he was caustic in his criticism of the outrageous cost of postage. This was a serious complaint throughout the area and certainly did not originate with him. It was not so much a criticism of the postal service but of the express offices that added a charge, causing each letter to cost twenty-five cents for delivery. Postmaster McClure disliked the professor even before he discovered the pedagogue's role as the Observer.

McClure had been involved in an early duel in the area and was wounded by R. W. Whitsitt. One can imagine how humiliating it was for him to have two hundred people watch his defeat, then to know that they were speculating about the extent of his wound. No doubt he was offended when the Observer made glowing comments about Whitsitt, a leader in the town land company.

McClure was good friends with steamboat captain W. H. Parkinson. When Parkinson involved himself in an episode of claim jumping, the whole settlement got involved. Parkinson and some of his men decided to build on a lot that belonged to the town company. The lot was unoccupied, and the group figured to build on it and thus claim it for themselves.[103]

When Whitsitt and his entourage sallied forth to challenge this land grab, they were met with the barrels of rifles. They retreated. A group of citizens numbering about eighty met to discuss how they could protect their investment in the town company lots without resorting to an open gunfight. At one point Mayor John Moore was sent to parlay with the jumpers. He returned to report that they were heavily armed and had no intention of leaving the property. They continued to build.

Meetings resumed. Some in the group wanted to storm the site and retake the property at gunpoint. Another quieter plan emerged in which several men went to the site at night, tore down the construction, and destroyed the lumber. The jumpers were infuriated. One of them followed Whitsitt with a rifle but failed to get off a shot. Parkinson was so angry that he took three shots at Major R. P. Bradford, fortunately missing each time.

Excitement throughout the city was at a fever pitch. Writing as the Observer, Goldrick included a piece in his column in the *Missouri Democrat* telling about the situation. He was not personally involved in any of this except as a Denver observer who wrote anonymously for the eastern paper. During the midst of the melee the Observer wrote:

> *Some scoundrels would jump Pike's Peak itself, or even the whole Rocky Mountains, if they only thought they could get other scoundrels to help them hold them. . . . If designing thieves and traitors think they can eventually get far ahead of our Town Company officers, they will bark up the wrong tree sooner or later.*[104]

While the citizens were meeting to further discuss how to deal with the bullying, gun-toting jumpers, word came from Parkinson offering to relinquish claim to the property in return for compensation for the lumber that was destroyed. This amicable solution brought the turmoil to an end, or so it was thought.

When McClure's enemy, Whitsitt, managed to settle the affair with Captain Parkinson legally, the Observer reported on the resolution:

> *At a meeting of citizens . . . a written proposition was received from Capt. Parkinson . . . and others, proposing to make peace and relinquish their jumping claim on the Denver town-site.*[105]

That should have ended the matter; however, McClure continued to seek the identity of the Observer. He would not be satisfied until he reaped his vengeance. What transpired after several months was strange, indeed, in view of the fact that Parkinson had settled in favor of the town company and relinquished his claim.

As it turned out, McClure continued to harbor deep offense at what the Observer had written months before, and brooded about the need to get even. He vowed to identify and then bring great harm to the correspondent. He was already angry at the Observer for the antislavery, pro-Union comments, and also for the favorable comments about his mortal enemy, Whitsitt.

Considering the climate of the times, the professor's desire for anonymity reflected more common sense than cowardice. The territorial government seemed unable to provide protection against gun-toting rowdies who roamed the streets. Goldrick refused to carry either a gun or a knife and was an easy target for bullies. Perhaps if he had realized that his life depended on the Observer remaining anonymous, he would have been more careful. He wrote in a fun-loving fashion, attempting to express the sentiments of the community in a manner that was appealing and stimulating to readers. He went too far. When he carelessly left town to tour the mines, both as Goldrick and as the Observer, he gave himself away.

The postmaster's suspicions and his fury were heightened. What followed was recorded in newspapers in the region and in the East. A good account was in the *Philadelphia Inquirer*. The article was unsigned but written by the correspondent to the *New York Tribune*, possibly their venerable correspondent A. D. Richardson. He wrote:

> *Denver City, Nov. 6, 1860 — For the last few days Denver has been the scene of a fresh excitement. Some months ago, P. W. [W. P.] McClure, Postmaster of this city and Chief Justice of Jefferson territory under the Provisional Government, took umbrage at a statement made in the St. Louis* Democrat *by I. J. [O. J.] Goldrick, a correspondent of that paper, and attaché of the* Rocky Mountain News. *The statement I am assured*

was true, but McClure compelled Goldrick, at the muzzle of his revolver, to sign a complete and humiliating retraction. That Goldrick, under the persuasive influence of a cocked pistol in the hand of an intoxicated man, should have signed that or any other paper, was not remarkable; but instead of properly exposing and denouncing the outrage, when set at liberty, he refrained from giving publicity to it. From this silence McClure drew the natural inference that he could bully Goldrick to any extent, and since that time, when under the influence of liquor, he has frequently made demonstrations upon him, which have terrified him exceedingly, and kept him in constant fear of his life. One evening last week, in a ball in the Tremont House, his menaces were of such a character that Goldrick fled to an apartment, locked himself in, and only succeeded in making his escape after several hours, when McClure had been seduced away from the foot of the stairs for the purpose of having a drink.[106]

The note Goldrick had been forced to sign earlier at gunpoint was as follows:

Sir—During the past winter, in my letters to the Missouri Democrat *I misrepresented Capt. Wm. H. Parkinson, at a time when he most needed truth to back him. I acknowledge that the assertions, which I made, in that paper, in respect to him, were false.*[107]

The professor was terrified enough to sign just about anything. McClure was drunk, had his rowdies with him, and was quite capable of pulling the trigger.

McClure published the "confession" in the *Rocky Mountain Herald*, a paper in competition with the *News*. Goldrick responded with an announcement in the *Rocky Mountain News*:

Now what I want to say to the citizens of Denver and the orderly public here . . . is that I never have written anything

*false or personally injurious to Capt. Parkinson, and that W. P.
McClure corralled me one evening . . . with that paper written
out, commanding me to sign it at once. . . . The only thing that
ever was published about Capt. P. in the St. Louis* Democrat *was
an article during the month of February last.*[108]

Leaving out the more inflammatory parts, Goldrick repeated the
text of his Observer article about claim jumpers, trying not to damage
Parkinson further, in view of his fair settlement with the land company.
Goldrick added:

*Now, the above is the head and front—the all and the total—
that Mr. McClure, or anybody else, can show up, or prove, or
present against the writer, and this, altogether, was no more than
a plain brief item of current public news.*[109]

This public admission by Goldrick that he was indeed the Observer
of the *Democrat* sent McClure into yet another rage. It was two days
later, at the social event at the Tremont House, that the vengeful
postmaster threatened to kill Goldrick. The professor used his pen to
fight for his life. On the front page of the *News* he wrote:

*I repeat my heart and soul's solicitation to the good people
of this city, to secure matters in such a way that a character who
behaves so outrageous and unsafe shall not cut off my life any
dark moment.*[110]

The citizens had previously formed a city government and had
appointed a vigilante committee to keep the peace, but the ruffians did not
recognize it, claiming that they only recognized the territorial government.
In an attempt to protect himself, Goldrick filed charges against McClure.
In response, the postmaster refused to recognize the local law and locked
himself in the post office, with his armed friends standing guard.

William Byers showed good judgment by broadening the issue. In
the *News* he wrote:

> *Citizens, Attention!—Let it be remembered that the struggle in which our city government is now engaged, is no longer an issue between W. P. McClure and O. J. Goldrick, or any other individuals, but is, in reality, an issue between the city government and the outlaw element, against which the better class of citizens has been compelled to contend for more than a year past.* [111]

McClure held out for two days, but on the third day, with the crowd of concerned citizens swelling in the street, he surrendered and posted bond. This event was important in the early history of Denver, not because Goldrick's life was spared, but because local government and a vigilante committee appointed by them prevailed in establishing a semblance of local law and order. [112]

The professor had sent off his September Observer letter to the *Democrat*. After reading this article, no one could accuse him of being a booster.

> *There are so many fast men and women, gamblers . . . and broken down institutions around who appear to "toil not, neither do they spin," that it seems to affect a great many of those persons who came out here as bonafide workers. . . . Thousands in the mining towns, as well as this large city of Denver, are complaining of the "dullness of times," and the "tightness of the money market." If times do not shortly improve, things will collapse pretty certainly this fall and winter, among both big and little fishes.* [113]

In October he ended his zestful time as the Observer. The fun had gone out of writing the column. Goldrick's last Observer letter in the *Missouri Democrat* was published on October 11, 1860. He finished by saying, "There is no safety here to personal life or personal liberty, almost, when these rascals have grown excited on a bust." The professor had written the column for eleven months and seen his words reproduced widely in eastern newspapers. The popularity of his work had been gratifying.

When the Civil War started, McClure left the area and joined the Confederate forces. He was part of a group of rebel soldiers who attempted to return to Colorado to encourage sympathy for the South. His unit was massacred by Osage Indian scouts working for the Union.[114] Though no one wished such a fate for any man, it was hardly surprising that McClure met a violent death.

Chapter 6

The War Years

Though the war would soon play havoc with their lives, by the time it started, the citizens had made some progress in the educational system. After closing the school during the coldest part of 1860, Goldrick reopened in May in better quarters. In December the *Omaha World Herald* reported on the progress:

> *The first school in the gold fields, opened a year ago by Prof. O. J. Goldrick in a one-room, mud-roof log cabin on Blake Street, is flourishing. When it opened it had 13 pupils, described as "two Indian, two Mexican, and the rest white and from Missouri." Today it has 30 students.* [115]

The professor hired a bright young lady from Iowa to assist him. During this time, two new schools opened with women teachers. Indiana Soris, principal of one of the new schools, spoke favorably of Goldrick's teaching ability.[116] When a movement to establish a public school system got underway, Goldrick provided leadership. He encouraged the movement, speaking on behalf of the idea. On one occasion, he leapt on a packing crate in front of the Lindell Hotel and made a public plea.[117]

The citizens did not hold his Observer column against him. They apparently knew that their popular teacher was trying to write material of interest to both his readers back East and to the local citizens. At the end of 1861, he was elected superintendent of the newly created public school system for Arapahoe County.

At about that time, the citizens were glad to see the Apollo Hall upgraded and opened as the People's Theater. The professor was asked to give an opening presentation, so he mounted the stage and recited a poem that he wrote for the occasion. One can tell by the way the poem ends that, though Goldrick was repelled by guns, he was willing to take a stand with his pen when it came to preserving the Union. As was the custom of the day, the poem was quite long, so only the first and last stanzas are printed here. It is easy to imagine the professor in his fine full-dress suit, shining patent-leather shoes, silk cravat, and matching gloves as he mounted the stage to speak in his clipped Irish brogue:

Pike's Peakers! All! From whatever climes,
You've crossed the Plains, to see or search the mines,
We greet you! Here tonight!
And bid you welcome to the sight,
And sound of what may on this People's stage be
To present Virtue bright, or cause you vice to shun,
To show up nature's traits,—shoot folly as it flies,
And catch the manners, living, as they rise!
From Shakespeare's genius, and Ben Johnson's power,
To grow and gladden, like the mead with showers,
as their high strains of inspiration roll,
Cheer up the heart and elevate the soul,
And to your heart, and soul, and ear, and eye,
Teach beauty, truth, and love, and melody.

We greet you here tonight, on Colorado's plain.
From every section of our vast domain.
Here, where as yet, we stand alone on squatter's rights,
But stand, as yet, thank God, beneath the stars and stripes!

Here on this highway between the East and West,
'Neath peaks and mountains, from whose snowy crest,
The air of freedom, like the grace of God,
Falls on the citizen, and fructifies our sod,
Dispels Disunion and its impious band,
From off this backbone of Columbia's land,
Here where our Gilpin, many years gone by,
Foretold our future with a prophet's eye,
And where young Fremont—this pathfinder bold,
With patriotism buoyant, and bravery yet untold,
Paved out the way for pioneers—for nations yet to come
Where, through God's aid, shall ever wave the flag of Washington![118]

The professor served as superintendent in 1862–63. By then the war was raging and the population was unstable due to citizens leaving to fight. Sufficient funding for school construction did not materialize, but still, after dividing Arapahoe County into school districts and using resources that he had, Goldrick established Colorado's first public school system in rented space.[119] During his tenure, he prepared for the population growth that would come by holding examinations of twenty individuals and gave ten of them certificates of qualification as teachers.[120]

During the time that Goldrick was organizing the schools, he continued moonlighting as city editor for the *News*. After writing some freelance articles for Byers during the early months following his arrival, he was hired as a managing editor in 1863 and continued working for the paper until April of 1865.[121]

The Civil War engulfed the area with strong sentiments. Beginning in August of 1861, Territorial Governor William Gilpin organized an infantry. He issued scrip to buy provisions for his troops. The store owners gladly supplied the needed goods, only to learn later that the scrip was not redeemable. Gilpin had issued it without getting approval from the federal government. Turmoil followed when storekeepers tried to redeem the notes.[122] News of the course of the war in the main theaters was spotty and always several days after the fact, because telegraph service to Denver did not arrive until late in 1863.

Goldrick's brother William's diary has a gap from missing pages between 1854 and the end of 1872. William's descendants say that the pages existed prior to the 1960s. Someone apparently removed them from the diary. Joan Marie Goldrick Johnson, William's great-great-granddaughter and the one who carefully transcribed the diary, said that the precious family record was being sent around to various cousins, and it turned up with the binding loose and pages missing. Everyone back down the line who had seen the diary said that it was that way when they got it. The diary was rebound without the missing pages.[123]

When the entries resume in 1872, William is railing against his daughter Susan. She had eloped, had a bad marriage, divorced, and returned home with her child. It is doubtful, however, that her actions would have caused the pages to be removed. She was a child in 1854 when the lost pages began. Unfortunately, the gap makes it impossible for us to know what William thought of the professor's activities in Colorado and what he thought of the Civil War.

We do know that William was opposed to slavery in all its forms. Many years before the war, he read *Slavery in America: A Narrative of the Life and Adventures of Charles Ball, a Black Man*. In his diary, he noted that he "read most of the narration of Chet Ball. If it is true, American slavery truly is the vilest that ever saw the sun." By the time the war started, William and his family had settled permanently in Delaware County, Ohio. His son and namesake, William, served for a time in the Union's 85th Ohio Infantry.[124]

In spite of the war that tore Denver apart, the pioneers who remained continued their enterprises as best they could. Shipments from the East were often delayed or interrupted, causing the newspapers to be printed on wrapping paper or any paper the pressmen could get their hands on.

When Goldrick's term as school superintendent expired at the end of 1863, he gave up pedagogy and became a full-time newspaper man.

Throughout his life, he remained a strong supporter of public schools. As a journalist, he often wrote about school matters.

The years went by swiftly, and with the arrival of the telegraph lines in October of 1863, the news of the war could be reported with more efficiency, though at times the lines were torn down by Indians or bad weather and had to be repaired. The journalists stayed busy trying to keep the public informed, and also writing lighter material to give respite from constant worry.

One of Goldrick's most interesting assignments for the *News* was to travel throughout the Rocky Mountain West selling subscriptions and advertisements. While doing this, he posted letters and articles back to the paper, telling of towns and describing the countryside and the people.[125] Goldrick proved to be a good salesman of ads and subscriptions.

During this period, he showed that his strong curiosity and sense of adventure exceeded his fear of harm. On occasion, he would leave the stage at one of its stops, rent a horse, and ride off to investigate some small villages along the way. This was in the midst of the Civil War. Unscrupulous characters roamed the countryside, and yet Goldrick, with no gun and wearing his fine dress clothes, went on these lone excursions and wrote about what he saw.

An embarrassing incident occurred in 1863 that was caused by Goldrick's reluctance to resist the offer of a free drink when he was out on the town and ready for a party. He made himself look foolish, but no one seemed to hold it against him, and the pioneers enjoyed telling the story years later. One of his journalist colleagues wrote:

> *Talking with some of the old "barnacles" yesterday about the Professor, Captain John Maynard and Andy Stanbury recalled to mind a little incident which transpired in 1863 in what was called the old "Iambian" saloon on Larimer street, owned by Mr. Stanbury, and was then about the finest saloon in Denver. One evening the professor called there, while on route for a fancy dress*

party, and of course he was arrayed in his dress suit, lavender necktie, kid gloves, swallow-tailed coat and patent leather shoes.

While in the saloon a Frenchman named Ameil Berraud made some unkind remarks about the professor's attire, which, of course, was resented, and being urged by that famous comedian Mike Dougherty the professor challenged Berraud to mortal combat, and Dougherty was deputized to carry the challenge, which was at once accepted and pistols were chosen as the weapons at ten paces distance, Berraud in the meantime being let into the secret of the encounter. Captain Joe Maynard acted as second for Berraud and Dougherty for Goldrick. Dougherty, who was then playing in the old People's theater with that veteran actor Jack Langrishe, soon procured a brace of pistols from the theater, and loaded them with blank cartridges, prepared the combatants for the conflict in front of the bar in the saloon. At the word, "ready," when the command of "fire!" was given, both pistols were discharged, and the professor dropped to the floor a badly demoralized man.

In an instant Andy Stanbury threw a few drops of Stoughton bitters on the professor's shirt which greatly excited him, and when a surgeon was called a fly blister was administered to his side, which soon gave him relief. It was several days before the professor was let into the secret of the duel when it became the talk of the town, and made him one of the heroes of Denver.[126]

Other accounts of the story portrayed Goldrick accepting one free drink after another from Dougherty, while the actor prodded the professor to stand up to his tormentor. Goldrick would never have challenged anyone to a duel or touched a gun if he had not been intoxicated beyond his ability to reason. Though Goldrick occasionally got caught up in such follies, he managed during the war years to establish a public school system, travel on extensive canvassing tours for the *News*, and do a good enough job at the paper to earn a significant promotion.

The journalists wrote of the war, read about it, and waited to hear if their friends who had marched off to battle, both for the North and South, would return. Lives went on, amid concern for the country's future, joy over the arrival of the telegraph lines, and hope that someday soon, they would see the arrival of a railroad line.

On May 19, 1864, a great tragedy occurred. A flood swept away the *News* office and much of the city, killing twelve residents.[127] Sometimes a newsman's greatest scoop comes from being on hand when devastation occurs. Goldrick wrote a long, breathless, unedited account in the middle of the night, and since the printing press had washed downstream, Byers got his competing newspaper, the *Daily Commonwealth*, to print Goldrick's story on May 24.

This sweeping piece has been reprinted many times. The writing style was meant to give a sense of immediacy, as though one were there. The following is an excerpt from the body of the article:

> *Higher, broader, deeper and swifter boiled the waves of water, as the mass of flood, freighted with treasures, trees, and livestock, leaped towards the Blake street bridge, prancing with the violence of a fiery steed stark mad: "Fierce as ten furies, terrible as hell."*
>
> *Great God! and are we all "gone up," and is there no power to turn the tide was asked all round. But no; as if that nature demanded it, or there was need of severe lesson it teacheth to the citizens of town, the waves dashed higher still, and the volume of water kept on eroding bluffs and bank, and undermining all the stone and foundations in its rapid course.*

The flood account would meet with the approval of some modern environmentalists and philosophers. The professor wrote:

> *Men are mere ciphers in creation; at least the chattels of the elements and the creatures of circumstance and caprice. While worldly fortune favors, they think of naught but self, care little for*

the laws of nature and care less for nature's God! Providential warning will alone affect them, when their wellbeing and their wealth are affected at the same time. . . . Had we continued settling Cherry Creek as we commenced, and thoughtless of the future, see what terrible destruction would have been our doom, in a few years more, when the waters of heaven, obeying the fixed laws, would rush down upon us and slay thousands instead of tens.

During this time, with the war reaching a crescendo, Goldrick's brother Thomas came to America. His timing was bad. Life was not as easy in America as he had imagined, and he soon became disillusioned. He wanted to return home. In his anxiety, he became quite ill. Brother William had his hands full with his large family and a medical practice. When Thomas was well enough to travel, William's father-in-law, Dr. Halderman, took the situation in hand. He and some of his friends collected money to send Tom back to Ireland.[128]

William heard from him during the time of Sherman's devastating march through the South. Thomas had made it home but complained bitterly that a rascal had stolen most of the money and left him just enough to get home. He said someone in the ship ticket office had sold him a false ticket that was worthless and then had run off with his money. When he got back to Sandfield, he had found that their mother was quite ill. He asked William to forward his letter to James, hoping for money from their ever-dependable brother.[129]

A few weeks later, James received a letter from Thomas. He thanked James for the money he had sent and apologized. He blamed their mother for having encouraged him to go to America, and said that when he got home, he had found that their sister Ann had sold the cow, heifer, mare, and foal, and then spent the money. Apparently by the time Thomas got back to Ireland, their mother was living on borrowed money. Even in the task of looking after her aging mother, Ann proved to be a poor manager, causing more problems than she solved. All of this created more challenges for James to solve.[130]

The professor was hundreds of miles away in Denver when all of this was going on. James saved the letters that provided the account of this sad escapade. Another letter he saved—a notice about a mortgage he held on a farm—gives a glimpse of James's good management skills. The farm owner sold the farm and offered James the full payment of the loan, plus any pending interest, or the option to allow the note of debt to James to continue for another three years at 6 percent interest, with additional land the man owned as collateral.[131] James husbanded his resources well and used those resources openhandedly to help his family.

Goldrick's flood story must have earned him a spot near the masthead of the *Rocky Mountain News*. When the paper resumed its regular publication after the flood, it listed him as associate editor.[132]

A year later, Goldrick was ready for a new challenge. The divisive war was finally over, and he wanted a new start that would give him more control of a newspaper. He had learned a great deal about the region by traveling and writing for the *News*, and had proved to himself that he could sell ads and subscriptions. He also knew that he could produce reams of material to fill the pages of his own paper. Goldrick sought a spot farther west where he could be an editor-owner, or part-owner. It was with a sense of nostalgia that he left his friends at the *Rocky Mountain News*. They surprised him by giving him a fine going-away gift, and then recorded the event in the paper.

A pleasing incident occurred in our office this afternoon, in the shape of a presentation to Professor O. J. Goldrick, late local editor of the News and long and favorably known to everybody in the West. The gift was a superb gold # 9 Faircloth pen with a solid native gold handle manufactured to order by A. B. Ingols of this city, and appropriately engraved with the inscription, "Presented to O. J. Goldrick by the Proprietors and Typos of the News office, Denver, May, 1865." The presentation in behalf of the office was made by C. L. Fowler in a short and happy speech and was most graciously received by the "Professor," but speech making not being in his line, and fearing that he might not do the subject justice if he attempted it, a few bottles of champagne and things came at his bidding, and all hands had a good, convivial time. Mr. Goldrick takes with him to his new home the best wishes of all connected with the News.[133]

His friends were, of course, being factious about his speech making. All concerned knew that he could make a speech at the drop of his top hat. But their warm wishes were quite sincere. They encouraged and followed his career and readily printed some of his freelance articles after he had left the *News*. Byers remained a lifelong friend.

Chapter 7

Editor — Proprietor

Believing that opportunity awaited him in Salt Lake City, Goldrick journeyed there to become associate editor of the *Daily Union Vedette*. The newspaper had started as a small sheet published by and for the soldiers at Fort Douglas and the nearby areas. The word *Vedette* is French and is defined as a sentinel on horseback on the outskirts of an army, watching for trouble. Being the voice of that sentinel undoubtedly appealed to Goldrick.[134]

When he arrived in Salt Lake City, he found that the paper was in need of improvements. He solicited subscriptions heavily from the military personnel throughout the region and traveled into nearby areas, successfully enlarging the circulation. Shortly after his arrival, he expanded the paper to six columns and improved the typography.

Goldrick introduced his thoughts on editorializing. "Time has both hallowed and abused the custom of saying something Salutatory, when commencing enterprises editorial. The writer has a theory about the matter which differs from most of his 'illustrious co-temporaries.' It is that performances—not promises—are more befitting a paper paragrapher, leaving time, which can tell all things, to 'define his position,' and display his talents, if he's got 'em!"

The editorials he wrote drew immediate attention for their scathing condemnation of polygamy. Though the paper, which was aimed primarily at the Gentile population, had published many articles challenging the practice, the former writing had lacked the thrust and jab of Goldrick's pen.

Reprisals soon followed. When one of the newspaper carriers rode his horse on the sidewalk in the city, he was fined ten dollars, and yet Mormons on horseback could do the same thing with no penalty. Some of the former editors had tried to remain anonymous for fear of reprisals. Though Goldrick did not sign his articles, he did not hide. The paper had an office where people could order advertisements and purchase subscriptions. Notices such as the following were published: "Residents and transient citizens wishing job work, advertising, or subscription, will be promptly waited upon by applying to O. J. Goldrick at the temporary branch office." Presumably, the professor believed that with Fort Douglas nearby, ample protection was available so that the *Vedette* could function as an open and independent newspaper.

Subscriptions increased rapidly. Though the *Vedette* was supposedly banned from Mormon households, it thrived as the only non-Mormon newspaper in the region. Readers responded to the improvements that the new editor made.

One problem that the professor addressed was that of subscribers of long standing who were lax in payment. He wrote:

> *Pay up.—For months and seasons past our city agent has been easy to a fault with scores of friends and patrons in the matter of collecting. With the present poor facilities for getting paper, ink and printing material from the East, at former freight, and indeed at any figure, we must be just before we are generous, and put in force our published terms 'invariably in advance' for subscriptions without respect of persons. Every pound of this white paper stands us One dollar and fifty cents, first cost and coach freight delivered.*[135]

The professor may not have realized that he was using an old proverb in this entreaty: "We must be just before we are generous." In his profligate youth, his own father had written to him and admonished him with those very words, encouraging the young pedagogue to live within his means.[136]

Goldrick believed that his tenure in Utah was successful, but he did not enjoy living in the hostile environment that his anti-polygamy articles engendered. Reports filtered from the Tabernacle that the *Vedette* was being called a vile, dirty, nasty sheet that should no longer be tolerated. By the end of 1866, the professor was ready to leave Utah. The following dispatch was printed in the *Rocky Mountain News*:

> *A terrible state of affairs is prevailing in Utah. Dr. Robinson was decoyed from his bed recently, on pretense of needing his medical services and brutally murdered in the streets of Salt Lake. O. J. Goldrick informs us that there is no safety of property or life for Gentiles in Mormondom and that the government does not furnish the protection necessary to ensure a better state of things. The* Vedette *has changed hands and is now published by P. L. Shoaff and Co. General Connor has telegraphed Rev. Norman McCleod, who has been east on a visit that it is unsafe for him to return to Salt Lake during the present state of affairs.*[137]

Many years later, one of the professor's Colorado colleagues wrote about his time in Utah:

> *In the early part of 1866 Professor Goldrick went to Salt Lake City, where he became connected with the* Daily Vedette, *a sprightly sheet especially conducted in the Gentile interest, and to its editorial columns he contributed some of the most scathing articles ever written against polygamy. Prior to assuming the editorial chair of the* Vedette *he was sent on a canvassing tour for the paper to the mining camps of Idaho and Montana, and the best descriptive articles concerning these regions were from his pen.*[138]

After leaving Utah, Goldrick's next effort was as proprietor-editor in Black Hawk, Colorado, throwing in with a man named Henry

Garbanati. Their paper, the *Daily Colorado Times*, was a struggling operation. They tried hard to extend their subscriptions and soon realized that most of their subscribers and advertisers were from Central City. They relocated there, but the future did not look bright enough for Goldrick. After a few months, he sold out and left.[139]

During the time when he was trying to decide his next step, his brother Thomas sent another pleading letter to James. He accused Owen of not sending money that he had promised. The professor was, as a rule, generous, and it is impossible to know if this accusation was true, or a manipulative ploy on Thomas's part. Thomas told James that the newspaper James had sent was very clever, and he thought surely James had written it. This appears to be an attempt to flatter his generous brother. The newspaper was most likely one of Owen's from Black Hawk or Central City.

Thomas went on to announce that he had received a letter from their brother John's wife. The family knew very little about her and the children. John seldom mentioned them in his sparse letters home. She told Thomas that John had died from the overuse of alcohol and left her with the five children. She wanted James's address in America. Thomas assured James that he had not sent the address. Thomas's protectiveness toward James may have been prompted by his desire to protect his own source of help.[140]

Meanwhile, Goldrick's friends at the *News* continued to print his writing. One example is a review in his *Daily Colorado Times* of a lecture series he attended that was presented for the Miners and Mechanics Board in Central City. Goldrick's review of a lecture by a Mr. Yonley was reprinted in the *News*:

> *If they have any more impractical and antisonant* [sic] *efforts, we want to know it in advance so as to worry out the hour elsewhere. To be sure the speaker "exhausted the subject," so to speak; but he exhausted the audience at the same time. Some of the latter (who were not too lazy to laugh in their sleeves),*

went to sleep or "stood horizontally in their pews."

We did think J. B. Wolff's highfalutin dissertation on scalene triangles and complex-gendered mules were mighty rich, but Yonley's material midwifery is richer; and perfectly peals the bark from the oaks of transendalism [sic] *and old Swedenborg himself at the same time.*[141]

The professor returned to Denver and found the opportunity he was seeking. The *Rocky Mountain Herald* had been active in Denver, changed its name to the *Dailey Commonwealth,* then sold out to the *Rocky Mountain News* after the flood of 1864. Goldrick was able to buy equipment that he needed and to revive the paper as a weekly, using its original name. As proprietor and editor, he would be responsible for selling ads, encouraging subscriptions, and writing enough copy to fill the pages. He thought that a true revival of the paper was in order, so he numbered his editions as though the paper had only been asleep, not dead, by showing on the masthead that the paper began in 1860, which was when the original paper of that name had started. This project of owning and editing his own paper in the city he loved turned out to be a fortuitous decision.[142]

Chapter 8

The *Rocky Mountain Herald*

Before Goldrick printed the first paper under his editorship, he traveled far and wide to solicit advertisements and subscriptions. He knew people throughout the region from previous travels and was confident that he had enough support from the businesses and residents to begin his enterprise. During the months he was doing his canvassing for his own paper, he was fortunate that the *Rocky Mountain News* published some articles about his travels. This was a strong indication of support from his old colleagues, since he was selling ads and subscriptions for his paper in areas that he once canvassed for them. In one of his articles published in the *News*, he wrote extensively about agriculture.

> *A traveler through these counties of El Paso, Pueblo, Huerfano, Fremont and Los Animas, imagines himself transported to the old productive neighborhoods of Iowa or Ohio. He sees splendid stock and spacious dwellings, golden wheat fields, and square miles of corn everywhere he goes; with intelligent and enterprising farmers and families to possess them.* [143]

Even though he would soon be competing with the *News*, his former colleagues allowed him to tell their readers that they could soon read more of his reviews of the farming areas when his *Rocky Mountain Herald* got underway.

In another *News* article during this period, Goldrick suggested that Denver and the state's southern agricultural area were missing a great opportunity to trade with one another.

> *The eight or nine southern counties of Colorado with these three northerly counties of New Mexico, mostly all are obtaining their goods from Kansas City, Leavenworth, or St. Louis, by the "long-stretch" style of transfer, and at figures full as high as Denver houses can supply the same goods and deliver them within a couple of weeks, whether it be winter or summer. The hint is worth heeding. With the Union Pacific railroad right in sight of you.*[144]

His article went on to give the distances to each of the towns that could be supplied with goods, and provided assurances about the quality of the roads.

On February 1, 1868, the first issue of the *Rocky Mountain Herald* wholly owned by the professor was published. He made certain policy statements to his readers, letting them know what to expect. He declared it to be a paper for the people, "Independent in politics and everything else." He also reassured his advertisers:

> *Almost every county, city, farming settlement, mining camp, sutler store, hotel, and saloon in Colorado, northern, middle, and southern, the Cimarron country, and New Mexico, generally, has been thoroughly canvassed by the Editor in person, during the past five months. Also the settled portions of Dakota and Arizona. Hence we commence with the circulation both at home and through the territory that would seem incredible to believe but for the fact we have mentioned. For business men, at home and St. Louis and Chicago, our advertising columns offer extraordinary advantages to gain public patronage.*

He went on to tell his new customers, "We have said that the journal will eschew extended articles on partisanship and palaver for the sake of sectional or selfish ends. . . . We mean to make this paper from the start a welcome visitor and eventually a necessity—to the merchant's store and the miner's cabin; to our family hearth and the frontier homes."

A formidable task awaited him. He lined up help with the mechanical part and eventually enlisted a colleague, Halsey Rhoads, in connection with the business management end of it.[145]

Goldrick advertised his paper as far away as Massachusetts.[146] People back East were quite interested in what was happening in Colorado's mountains. His friends at the *News* continued to support his efforts by calling attention to an ad on the day it appeared:

> *No one will fail to notice the card of that famous "local" and journalist, O. J. Goldrick, esq., who proposes to start a weekly paper, to be called the* Rocky Mountain Herald. *It will be spicy and interesting, and of course everybody will advertise in it and subscribe for it. We wish the* Herald *and the editor a cordial success.*[147]

After the paper had been in circulation for several months, Goldrick placed an ad that had glowing endorsements for his paper. Frank Hall of the *Miner's Register* gave him a good quote to use, and Horace Greeley's endorsement was valuable because he was well known throughout the United States. He wrote, "The *Rocky Mountain Herald* is the most handsome, lively, spicy and generally interesting journal that has come within our knowledge, East or West."[148]

With the good wishes of his friends, Goldrick was off to a fine start. During the first few months, he wrote articles intended to solidify his subscription base. Also during this time, his brother James found himself temporarily without a teaching job. He must have contemplated returning to Ireland to be near his aging mother. By this time, James himself was aging. In response to this idea, he received a strange letter from Thomas. After expressing thanks to Owen, William, Clarissa, and James for the money they had recently sent, he strongly discouraged James from returning to Sandfield to live. It was as though Thomas did not want to have to care for an aging brother—the one who had done so much for him.[149] Fortunately, James's decision to stay in America soon rewarded him with another teaching job.

In 1870 the professor tried to take his paper to a new level by starting a daily edition. This endeavor lasted only a few weeks. He dropped the idea and continued publishing the *Herald* as a weekly for the remainder of his career.[150]

Goldrick found that an advantage of being editor as well as proprietor of a newspaper was that he was included in the train excursions where the railroad brass fêted editors royally as they introduced them to the positive features of their new rail lines. One of the finest events took place in early 1870 when A. B. Pullman treated the Denver-area editors to "Breakfast on Wheels." Eleven members of the press were welcomed to the elegant smoking car where Colonel John S. Loomis, president of the National Land Company, introduced them to Colonel Pullman.[151]

Both the Kansas Pacific Railroad from Kansas City to Denver and the Denver Pacific that took passengers on to Cheyenne had added Pullman cars. These elegant hotels on wheels featured the finest accoutrements.

After toasts by representatives of the press and a responding toast from Loomis, the men adjourned to the dining car to enjoy a fine meal—fruit from California, wine from France, game from the Rocky Mountain slopes, and mountain trout, along with numerous other delicacies.

Needless to say, the editors had good things to say about the Pullman brothers and their enterprise. Not only did the journalists appreciate the fine introduction to this outstanding service, they understood how much the railroad and its refinements meant to the further development of the West and to their Denver home.

On a business trip to Kansas City, Goldrick had an opportunity to be rocked to sleep in a fine Pullman car. The following morning, as the train sped along through the plains, he heard gunshots. Making his way to the lounge car, he looked out the window at a sea of buffalo. Thousands of animals with their furry humps undulated as they stampeded alongside the train—buffalo as far as the eye could see. Men were hanging out of the train windows, shooting them for the sport of it. After the train passed the herd, bones and carcasses along the track made evident that this was a routine sport for travelers. Goldrick also saw large numbers of beautiful, graceful antelopes that met the same fate when they ran too close to the train.[152]

Owning his own newspaper expanded Goldrick's business and social activities. The opening of the Denver and Rio Grande Railroad offered editors another fine excursion. Invitations were extended to all editors of the territory, and they eagerly accepted the opportunity to travel on the train line's inaugural trip from Denver to Colorado Springs.[153]

The excursion train left Denver at eight in the morning with the engine *Montezuma* doing the heavy work of pulling the baggage car, a smoking car, and two elegant passenger coaches that the railroad moguls had named *Denver* and *El Paso*. The journalists soon found themselves speeding through the valley of the Platte past cultivated fields dotted with fine farms. The cottonwoods, resplendent in their fall colors, and the mountains as a backdrop gave the travelers a memorable view. When the train began the ascent toward the Great Divide, the scenery changed quickly, and they were surrounded by deep gorges outlined with huge spikes of rock in fantastic shapes.

The variety and picturesque beauty of the route impressed everyone on board. Passengers were gratified to see rich agricultural areas that the railroad would help in getting their fresh produce to markets. Also, they saw thousands of board-feet of fresh-cut timber piled along the way, waiting for transport. At Plum Station, they passed a freight train with eighteen cars loaded with lumber and supplies to help build Colorado's rapidly growing cities.

They arrived at Colorado Springs at one o'clock, enjoyed a sumptuous meal, and then were joined by General W. J. Palmer, president of the line. He was accompanied by former governor A. C. Hunt, who had been identified with the line since its inception.

With Palmer in the lead, they toured Colorado Springs and Colorado City by carriage. As dusk came upon them, they drove through the Garden of the Gods and were stunned by the beauty around them. From there they were driven to the famous boiling soda springs at Villa la Font, where they spent the night in fine accommodations. The next morning, they revisited the Garden of the Gods on their way back to the train in Colorado Springs that would return them to Denver.

The developing railroad lines spared no expense in introducing the press to their services. Railroad building was a competitive business, with many investors to keep happy. Glowing reports from the press, as well as political support, were important. The excursion to Golden in February of 1872 is an example of how the Colorado Central Railroad sought to entertain and inform.[154]

Only three editors were invited on this excursion. Goldrick represented the *Herald*, Byers represented the *News*, and Leonard represented the *Tribune*. Other guests were Governors Evans, Gilpin, and Hunt, along with several key legislators. Wives, daughters, and lady friends were also included in the group.

The atmosphere on the train from Denver to Golden was festive. When they arrived, some stayed in town to be entertained, while others were driven in carriages up the eight-mile grade to the site where men were dynamiting through the mountain. The visitors were able to see firsthand the seemingly impossible task of building a rail line through the mountains.

They returned to Golden, rejoined the rest of the party, and were fed a fine feast. Music was provided, and the party danced the night away before retiring to comfortable accommodations provided by the Golden Hotel. According to Goldrick, the event was a smashing success. He quoted a colleague from the *Colorado Transcript* who said, "There were practical railroad men in the party who expressed surprise and agreeable disappointment at the excellence of the work and the practicability of the line adopted, as nearly all of our Territorial papers even, had formerly contended that a railroad up this canyon was utterly impracticable."[155]

The professor was extremely busy at this time in his life. He was fortunate to have a brother who would and could address the problems back in Sandfield.[156] James made a trip back home at the time of their aging mother's death. After he settled things there, he returned to America. That left Ann and Thomas in Ireland, and James, William, and Owen all doing well in America.

As the owner and editor of an influential newspaper, Goldrick was offered favors from business owners who wanted to curry the approval of the press. Offending advertisers was a concern for any publication that relied on ads for revenue. Even so, the professor wrote what he thought needed to be said, without concern for any repercussions. His negative view of lotteries is a good example. Though these games were quite popular, and though Goldrick allowed the placement of lottery ads in his paper, he expressed his disdain for continuous games of chance that preyed on false dreams rather than encouraging hard work.[157]

In that era, lotteries abounded and were unregulated scams that hid the identity of the owners and the number of tickets sold. Goldrick strongly objected to a system whereby numbered tickets were printed using worthy causes to encourage sales, but no accounting was ever provided of how much money was given to the poor or, in one example, to the community musical enrichments that a lottery in question supposedly funded. Finding these lotteries fraudulent, he challenged other newspapers to speak up:

> *The public press—if true to its trusts and unsubsidized . . . should be the public's protector and conservator, and is so acknowledged in every free country at the present day. . . . That which is, above all, expected and duly demanded of the press, is its unfaltering faithfulness to the people and to the honest interests*

of the community, against all schemers, cheats or danger to their welfare, life or morals. The press which, for patronage, ignores an outrage or allows an injury on its community, ought to merit the condemnation of mankind, if not deserve the damnation of God!

Goldrick offered space in his paper to any lottery promoter who wanted to speak up and explain the legitimacy of his game. He dared them by saying that if they did not speak up and explain their games, profits, and gifts to charities, then "their scheme is unsafe."

A few years later, Goldrick appears to have softened his view. In 1881 he allowed large headlines on the front page of his paper advertising the Colorado State Lottery, managed by the Colorado Land and Mineral Association.[158] The accompanying article by A. B. Miller, one of the lottery managers, declared that this game had an "inviolable franchise conveyed in special charter granted by the Legislature of Colorado" and recognized "its obligation to the buyers of its tickets, and their rights to know that drawings are fairly made, what prizes are drawn, and by whom, and all other particulars. . . . It has nothing to conceal, and invites the closest scrutiny." Miller went on to say, "Lists of prizes will be published in the *Rocky Mountain Herald* and other papers of Denver after each drawing."

The professor's criticisms had not suppressed lotteries, but his strongly expressed views may have been instrumental in discouraging scams in favor of a game that was well regulated and open.

During the early 1870s, to the dismay of Owen and his brothers, Ann decided to move to America. Her children were grown and on their own. She was not trained to do anything except manual labor and found employment doing domestic work in Columbus, Ohio. William worried in his diary about her family being so scattered.[159]

Throughout his career, the professor either ignored criticism or responded with mild, sarcastic rebuttals. One criticism sent him into a fierce and condemning editorial rage. The critic had not attacked

Goldrick but had made fun of the Association of Colorado Pioneers, calling its members "veritable bummers and whisky-soaked veterans of '59." When the professor read this "slander" written by S. G. Fowler in the *Sunday Mirror,* his editorial response was scathing.[160]

He denounced Fowler as a "swollen-headed scamp (whom Chicago spewed out of her mouth, and Valmont vomited onto Denver), who is permitted to live off our big hearted pioneers whom he, with base ingratitude, abuses." Goldrick listed prominent members of the pioneer group, outstanding citizens who were longtime founders and leaders of Denver and Colorado. He stated that these pioneers did not need him to defend them, and though they were well able to defend themselves, he felt the need to "check up this filthy Fowler and to ventilate his dishonest and dishonorable style of dead-beating and blackmailing, as he has been practicing, for a miserable livelihood." He went on to declare that Fowler was dirty, sneaky, and greasy.

Among the claims he made against Fowler were extortion and blackmail, stating that Fowler accepted kickbacks for writing that a mine claim was a good one. Goldrick went on to say that this "fraud on decent journalism" extorted money from ladies by threatening to write lurid stories (true or not) about them unless they paid him hush money.

Goldrick's catalogue of derogatory terms was exhaustive: defamer, blackguard, cotton-gloved beat of a Bohemian, prostitute, cabbage-head, newspaper nuisance, unmanly, cadaverous, liar, despised devil, and he-harlot.

These insults are quite extreme, and for Goldrick to call Fowler "cotton-gloved" was a true insult. Goldrick was never seen in anything but fine leather gloves. Though he was sympathetic toward the poor who had to wear cheaper cotton gloves—or no gloves at all—his slam at the "cotton-gloved" Fowler was an indication that in Goldrick's eyes, the critic of the pioneers was a cheap fraud.

Professor Goldrick owed much to the stalwart pioneers. As a member of the group, he had been active in the organization since its inception. These were the people who, back in 1859, had welcomed him warmly into their midst, included him in all of their civic and social activities, forgave him his bouts of alcoholic indiscretion, and gathered in the streets around the post office to force Park McClure to post bond and thus protect the pedagogue's life. The pioneers were his closest friends and supporters.

The professor felt a special affection for the pioneer women. Overlooking his idiosyncrasies, they had welcomed him to family dinners, tried to match him up with their daughters, laughed at his teasing prods about female fashion, and admired his honest love for the children in the community.

When pioneer banquets were held, it was invariably Goldrick who was called upon to provide a toast to the ladies. He was given no warning on a certain occasion, but rose, paused, surveyed the fashionably dressed ladies before him, and provided the toast:

> *The ladies—the pioneer ladies, God bless them. They were few in the early days when Wilder and Fred Soloman and myself came to Pike's Peak, and therefore looked the more charming to our bachelor eyes. I remember them in '59 when they wore no bustles or frills or banged their hair, and when dried apples were good enough for pies, and a calico dress was a joy to the family, they accepted the situation as it was and they never kicked.*[161]

In January 1881, the professor was on the program to speak about the lady pioneers before an audience of 450 members and guests at the pioneer association's annual banquet:

> *On every occasion or emergency it was almost always the pioneer ladies who gave the strongest and promptest proof of principle and devotion to every object of enterprise gotten up for the public good. With the men, well doing was in general the result of selfish calculation, and well-behaving was with them the result of restraint. But with our pioneer women, it was as*

impulse and as inspiration springing fresh from the heart. They created civilization here, by founding homes and hospitality. They fostered schools. They propped up our pulpits. . . . They planted charity for all. They were sociable and neighborly, although having come here from all sections of the then disrupting union, they met and mingled together as one sisterhood, for the sole interest of Colorado.[162]

Professor Goldrick's general attitude about women was similar to that of Professor Henry Higgins of *Pygmalion*: women should spend less time with concerns over their curls and crinolines and more concern for developing their souls and their brains. He did not blame women altogether for their intense interest in their appearance. The culture of the day made marriage the only secure route for a young woman. Goldrick believed that it was wrong for society to expect young men to be self-reliant as soon as possible, yet frown on young women for seeking employment and independence:

Women have been shut out from many branches of employment, and existing public sentiment, while considering it disgraceful for sons to live long in dependence on their fathers, is almost equally opposed to allowing these sons' sisters to do anything for a livelihood. . . . It is not necessary to adopt the theories of those advanced partisans who would endow women with all the privileges of citizenship, and place like responsibilities on both sexes. . . . As the case now stands with a large class of women, their destiny lies between a barely possible marriage and dependent maidenhood. . . . In short, the mass of girls should be taught to be self-supporting.[163]

Though the professor believed in encouraging working women, he made a joking comment about the newly minted female lawyers. "They can try their eloquence and powers of persuasion hitherto limited to some one man upon twelve men in a jury box. We are afraid this would be putting our jury system to a too severe trial, and even our judges, crusty old chaps as they generally are, might get their legal ideas slightly confused at times by the pleading of some fascinating advocate."[164]

The *Herald* was independent of influence from strong political pressure. However, Goldrick was committed to the views of the Democratic Party and at times expressed his thoughts.

> *The true party of the union is the democratic party; that party which seeks to heal, not to open afresh the old wounds of the war; that party which would remove the line of demarcation between the north and south, which the republican policy seeks to perpetuate; that party which honestly holds that all men are equally entitled to the protection of the laws; that party which demands that the military shall be rightly subordinate to the civil power of the government; that party which would legislate for the poor as well as for the rich, and not wholly in the interests of money capitalists; that party which practices instead of merely promising economy and reform.* [165]

It is possible that some of his fellow Democrats were dismayed by the professor's favorable comments about the powerful Republican William Byers. On one occasion, Goldrick wrote a piece in high praise of Byers, comparing him to "Fremont, Louis and Clark, and those other pioneers who paved the way to this western country and then stuck to it through thick and thin."[166]

In 1876 Byers had a good chance of being nominated as the Republican candidate to run for the position of the state's first governor. A self-inflicted scandal ruined his political aspirations. Byers was a prominent middle-aged married man whose wife was involved in many civic activities. His liaison with an emotionally unstable milliner began to unravel and, when Byers attempted to withdraw from the affair, his mistress became wild, loud, and threatening.

Byers's political opponents were delighted. Even though the press in Denver refrained from writing about it at first, the scandal was soon a story of notoriety all over the country. Byers had refused to be blackmailed into paying his former mistress to suppress the story. Because of the timing, Goldrick suspected that the whole episode might have been planned. He considered the milliner, Mrs. Hattie Sancomb, to be not only unstable, but sly. She knew how much Byers had to lose if he did not do her bidding. The professor avoided writing about it as long as he could, but when one-sided accounts against Byers began to appear, he responded:

> *Now that this social scandal has culminated (and naturally will keep culminating) into notoriety, at home and abroad, by sensational versions, and conglomerations of fancy and filthiness, casting obloquy all on one side, regardless of right, we therefore deem it our duty and professional pleasure to present the more plausible and impartial view of the case, as corroborated by the following facts which will speak louder than words, and tend to show the true animus of the exposé against the editor and owner of the* News, *on the plea of "injured innocence," virgin virtues.*
>
> *Understand us now definitely. We don't palliate the defendant, or defend the plaintiff, in this much mixed and melancholy case. We consider that Mr. Byers was a big fool to allow himself to become attached, intrigued or inveigled into any such entangling alliances with any such divorced woman, when he knew that she knew he wasn't a single man, but was, on the contrary, "just the oyster" for baiting and beating into blackmail or black misfortune.*[167]

He went on to present the evidence that Mrs. Sancomb was a divorcée who had previously been sued by her former husband for adultery. He published the threatening letters she had sent to Byers, and printed Byers's story of when he met the woman and how she had written to him and initiated the friendship. The professor summed up his assessment by saying that when revenge causes the virtuous woman to lose her good name, then she is as cattle chewing on the cud of blackmail. "Fight the devils with fire. Prevent the killing of a good, useful man, even though it chagrined and showed up the schemes of every damsel or dame in Denver and Golden combined. 'Them's our sentiments' on the subject, and we'll stick to them for a friend, who is otherwise worthy, while there's a toe to our boot or a type in our office."

Goldrick had a fierce sense of purpose and was much too quirky to be controlled by anyone. He generally tempered his criticism with humor, and seldom displayed the venom that he used against polygamists and against Fowler, who had dared to ridicule his beloved pioneers. He wrote the truth as he saw it about issues that presented themselves. In his more serious writing in his *Herald* about events of the day, his articles showed him to be "a forcible, trenchant writer . . . fearless and outspoken."[168] He stated his beliefs without concern for what other people thought. "As a writer, he was what might be known from his conversation, outspoken, terse, aiming directly at the mark no matter what intervened."[169]

He also included many lighthearted pieces meant to entertain, rather than inform. He wrote about bachelors, pioneer ladies' fashions, aging flirts, and working women, and covered the social and cultural events in Denver and the area. Ireland was remembered in lyrical descriptive prose, along with facts about its political struggles. Quite often, when he made a point about a subject of concern, he used sharp comments tempered by humor. For example, he was unhappy with the naming of some of Colorado's beautiful sites.

> *Prof. Hayden has the deplorable practice of naming Colorado peaks after his friends, so we now have a Hoar Mountain— named after the late Attorney General.*[170]

His thrust at the churches was also tempered with tongue-in-cheek humor:

> *The value of church property in this city doubles once in five years. The increase in Christianity doesn't double once in ten years. Which shows that our churches have a sharper eye to saving money than saving souls. This statement is a melancholy one, but we fear it is true.*[171]

Goldrick loved the theater and enjoyed writing theatrical critiques. On one occasion, he turned himself into a theater entrepreneur and managed a series of talks by P. T. Barnum, with speaking engagements in Central City, Denver, and Georgetown. In view of Barnum's subject, *How to Be Healthy, Happy, and Rich*, it is comical that on the night of the Denver engagement, the professor pocketed $247 from his management gig, while Barnum earned $75 for his talk.[172]

The professor often wrote about school matters. On one occasion, he chastised the school board candidates and their platforms.

> *Well, we have had an election for board of education in the two school wards of town the other day. The great qualification was anti-African miscegenation. Maybe we'll have a system of free schools after a while. Goodness knows that it is time that the public funds are turned to account.*[173]

He expressed the opinion that fathers who pressured their sons to go into fields for which they were unsuited and in which they had no interest accomplished nothing more than to create "moody and discontented men, entirely out of their sphere in their enforced vocation, and of little use in the world except as furnishing a warning to others by the conspicuous failure they have been."[174]

The support and funding of public schools was passionately supported by Goldrick. He believed that overcrowded, dilapidated school buildings and a high student-teacher ratio let the students know where their education stood in terms of public priorities. The appearance of the schools "almost invariably indicates the state of educational interest in the district." He believed that the citizens in the territory needed to support and embrace public schools if they hoped to thrive and attract those looking to make the area their home.[175]

He freely extolled his philosophy about classroom education. Children should have time to play. They should not be sent home with piles of homework.[176] He strongly endorsed free education for all students, along with funding for public, but not parochial, schools.[177]

When writing about his beloved Ireland, he did not denounce the Catholic Church. He believed that Catholics and Protestants should not waste energy fighting one another, but should join forces to free Ireland from the powerful grip of the money men in England. He was ahead of his time when he wrote, "Papacy and Protestantism will have to accord each other's rights, ere the reign of any Utopia on Irish soil."[178]

Like many other western editors, his initial sympathy for the Indian tribes gradually changed. After the Civil War, William T. Sherman was appointed to handle the challenge of managing the Indian population. Sherman wanted to herd them onto two reservations— one to the north, the other to the south—and gradually civilize them. Goldrick agreed that this plan was probably the only feasible one, yet he doubted that the Indians would accept it.[179]

By 1876, Goldrick and other editors were calling for the total subjugation of the native tribes. "From the British boundary on the north to the Rio Grande, murderings, scalpings and burnings are things of daily occurrence." He recommended that the army attack the Indians in winter when they were in their camps and not dispersed across the countryside, and that "it be briskly carried off, and without intermission, until every hostile band of Indians along the whole frontier has been thoroughly subdued."[180] The idealism and sympathy that Goldrick had expressed in 1860 about the "poor Indians" had disappeared.

When the professor began his *Herald*, he promised his readers an independent newspaper. He kept his promise. He could be influenced by friendships and loyalties, but not by patronage.

Chapter 9

The Best and Worst Years

Travel was a big part of the professor's editorial duties. He attended meetings and political events, and visited his advertisers. The most important trip of his life occurred in spring of 1873 on a visit to Chicago. It was there that he met the widow of D. C. Driscoll, the former city attorney for Chicago. Edith captivated his bachelor heart as no woman before or after. There was no coquetry about her. She was lovely, gracious, and keenly intelligent. After a short courtship, he surprised himself by asking her to be his bride. He was even more surprised when she accepted.

Edith Kenny Driscoll became Goldrick's wife in Chicago in a ceremony solemnized before Rector Charles Edward Cheney on May 1, 1873.[181] His old cohorts at the *Rocky Mountain News* got wind of the marriage over the wire service, contacted the *Herald* office to find out where Goldrick was staying, and then checked with the hotel to confirm that a Mr. and Mrs. Goldrick were registered. The next morning they broke the news to the citizens of Denver.

> *By our Chicago exchange, received last night, and by the hotel register of "O. J. G. and wife". . . The worthy Goldrick has "gone and done it" like a gallant gentleman as he is and ever has been after Colorado was "first settled." The professor's popularity and fame is already known too far and wide in this western country to need new praises from our pen. His bride has been*

one of the noble queens in Chicago's quiet society for a few years past, and, we judge, is gifted with both culture and common sense alike to grace a court or guild a cabin, as the vicissitudes of western life should chance to send. Her former husband was one of the ablest criminal lawyers in the northwestern state of the nation as per Wilkie's published book on the Chicago bar. . . . The present Mrs. G. is a sister to the Hon. T. J. Kenny, well-known by all Ohioans as the "eloquent senator from the Ashland district." We welcome back our friend Goldrick with his (such a) wife to our western metropolis. His hosts of friends will join with us in a "here's to your good health," etc., and "may they all live long and prosper."[182]

His bride received a fine reception by the Denver ladies. The pioneer families were gracious in fêting and welcoming her. What great good fortune it was for Goldrick that his wife was a modest lady who, in addition to living within her means, was bright, amiable, and able to participate in interesting discussions. The professor was proud to introduce this fine and worthy wife to his friends.[183]

In the years that followed, Goldrick's devotion to Edith gave his life a whole new texture. He readily dropped his bachelor habit of stopping by the bars. In fact, he gave up alcohol completely. The man who never confided in anyone now had a loving confidant. He called her his nearest and dearest friend. His life now revolved around Edith and his work at the newspaper.

The centennial year of our nation's birth, 1876, was one of the busiest and most productive years of Goldrick's life. The vote for Colorado to become a state had passed, and statehood awaited only President Grant's signature. The citizens decided to proceed with a Fourth of July statehood celebration while also celebrating the nation's centennial. The Colorado Pioneers appointed Professor Goldrick to its celebration committee,[184] and they planned a grand day of parades, music, speeches, a picnic, and fireworks. Since Goldrick was already writing a series of articles for the *Herald* telling the history of Denver, he was asked to be on the program and give an address on that subject.

The day of the celebration was warm and glorious. At sunrise, Denver bells rang throughout the city, as well as the blowing of whistles and the national salute of thirty-eight guns symbolizing the thirty-eight states of the Union. The parade formed early in the day, with bands, the governor's guard and other military units, the Colorado Pioneers wearing their armbands, and other fraternal organizations. Speakers and elected dignitaries rode in carriages. Members of the choral groups joined the parade. Storefronts along the route were festooned with patriotic red, white, and blue buntings.[185]

The most popular and exceptional display was a large float consisting of two connected wagons drawn by a team of decorated white horses. Lovely young Colorado ladies dressed to represent the thirteen original colonies, plus the additional states, all honored the first "Miss Colorado," the beautiful May Butler.

Fifty years later May Butler Brown remembered the occasion:

> *Proudly I sat upon the white wagon, decorated in bunting and flags of the United States. Teams of white horses drew the wagon up Larimer Street to Denver Grove, then a clump of trees on the bank of the Platte and the only thing in the city that resembled a public park. On all sides of me were other girls, each representing one of the states and all doing homage to their new sister Colorado. I wore a robe of bunting, high crown of gold and carried a golden wand in my hand. As the wagon proceeded through the streets cheer after cheer rose from the people of Denver and Colorado.[186]*

Governor John L. Routt gave a hearty welcome, which was followed by a reading of the Declaration of Independence by Mayor R. G. Buckingham. Goldrick was the next speaker. He summarized Denver's history, beginning with the first discovery of gold. He talked about the first marriage, the first birth, the complications of the forming of Denver City and Auraria, and the wise combination of the two cities. In general, he gave a history of the formation of the region. In his enthusiasm, he included an optimistic original poem.[187]

All hail to Colorado,
The Rocky Mountain gem!
That glistens on the summit
Of Columbia's diadem.
Here climate mild and varied
From plain to mountain dome,
Invites the poor from all the world
Who here can find a home.
With cattle on the thousand hills
And room for millions more;
With gold enough beneath to pay
The nation's debt twice o'er.

As usual, the professor injected a touch of humor. While enumerating the events and businesses that brought life to the city, he added, "We must not forget recording an event which happened here which made glad the hearts and the throats of thousands odd denizens of Auraria, on the 10th of November, 1859, to-wit, the establishment of a large beer brewery of Soloman, Tascher & Co. That beer, though quite drinkable, was as innocent of hops as our early whiskey was of wheat or rye."

Thirty years after the event, a reminiscence of that day by Major Jacob Downing, one of Denver's most distinguished pioneers, was published in the *Rocky Mountain News*. Downing was the first judge in Denver and recalled facts about early Denver that Goldrick did not mention.

"It was quite an elaborate celebration for those days," said
Major Downing. "It was a very noisy celebration—with fireworks
and considerable gun shooting. It was an extremely warm day.

I remember my wife was on the committee of the Ladies' Relief corps, which was to give the picnic in Denver Grove. She walked from Cherry Creek to Fortieth Street on Lawrence Street asking for donations for the dinner, and met with but one refusal, which shows you the generous instincts of our citizens of those days. The dinner was a great success, as was the entire celebration for that matter.

"You see, Denver had grown to be quite a town by that time. The vigilante committee had long since rid the town of any bad characters. I, as judge, sentenced 130 men to the chain gang in 125 days, I remember. Our policy was to let them escape if they wanted to—they never wanted to return to Denver. It was a respectable, law abiding peaceable town and one that anyone could have been proud to have lived in."[188]

Yes, they were a proud citizenry—especially the pioneers—for their early predictions had been realized to heights greater than expected. This high point in Goldrick's life was clouded by worry about Edith's health. His worry was justified.

He and Edith had enjoyed several good years of marriage. His paper was thriving, and he was in his prime. Though he was glad to have played an integral part in the great statehood celebration, he was anxious to get Edith to a specialist. For several weeks she had been losing weight, and a swelling in her abdomen did not look normal. At Goldrick's insistence, they made plans to visit the Philadelphia Exposition and World's Fair. A mock-up of the professor's first school was on display in Colorado's exhibit hall.[189] More urgent, and the central purpose of the trip, was their plan for Edith to consult a Philadelphia specialist.

It was evident that Edith was ill and losing ground. She was told what she and her husband feared the most. She had a large ovarian tumor that the physicians believed would surely prove fatal.[190]

Later, they traveled to New York, hoping the specialists there could offer an alternative prognosis. Edith was told that surgery was the only hope and that there was a slim chance of her surviving the operation. An intelligent and brave woman, Edith finally decided that she would take the slim chance of survival offered by surgery. While she was consulting with her doctors, Goldrick managed to locate his sister Ann, who was living in New York and doing domestic work. She planned to return to Ireland. He sent her address to his brothers who had lost contact with her.[191]

Edith was remarkable during the postoperative time. Realizing that she was dying, she carefully made disposition of her possessions. One of Goldrick's great-nieces says that family lore attributes some silver in the family to having come from Uncle Owen. "I know there was some beautiful silver in my grandfather's home that had once belonged to Owen."[192] Her grandfather was Dr. William Goldrick. It is doubtful that the professor, a bachelor most of his adult life, owned silver; however, Edith could have brought such items into the marriage, and on her deathbed, instructed that the silver be given to her sister-in-law, Clarissa Goldrick. Thus, the silver from Uncle Owen would continue to be possessed by his brother William's descendants.

Edith made things easier for her loved ones by planning her funeral. She had a favorite sister in Rhode Island and asked her husband and her family to bury her on the high bank on a shore there overlooking the sea. She died seven days after the surgery.

Rather than having to repeat the sad story of his loss to each of his associates in Denver, the professor sent an obituary tribute to the *Herald*, to appear shortly after he returned to Denver following her funeral.[193] He thanked the citizens for their gracious reception when she had moved there. He then explained the onset and progression of her terrible illness and her bravery. Always reticent about his private life, he spoke openly about his deep respect and love for Edith.

She felt that God, who was a God of love and wisdom and mercy had already blessed her and was about taking her to himself, after having fully chastened her and then forgiven her and sanctified her for another and better world to which she presently went, with the attributes of an angel and the confidence of a saint. . . . Her grave is on a green knole [sic] overlooking the sea . . . where the wild waves of ocean will chant vespers in her ear, until earth shall be no more.

It affords us the highest holiest pleasure to take the opportunity of testifying that the deceased was a woman of many great and good qualities. She would not tell a lie. She would not run to debt. She liked to live within her own and her husband's means. She hated hypocrisy, and abhorred gossip or tattle. Natural and noble, neat and high-toned, none knew her but to like her, nor named her but to praise, during her residence in this city. She was a person of great philosophy and force of character . . . she was a woman of brains, conscience . . . a true wife and a real lady, as such, so that for us, none but herself can ever be her parallel. May God be her guardian, and Heaven her home, forever and ever. Amen. O. J. G.[194]

Within a period of five years, Goldrick had lived through the high point and low point of his life. Brother William, who had lost most of his medical practice to old age, now wrote in his diary only once a year. In January of 1878 he wrote simply, "Brother Owen's wife died."[195] There are no family letters in the collection to tell us of communication between the brothers during this period. Sister Ann had returned to Ireland and was able to get a job there.[196] Thomas was still in Ireland, presumably farming. James continued to teach.

Though Goldrick's friends said that he was never the same after Edith's death, he was active enough in the events of the day to be nominated by the Democratic Party to run for Superintendent of Public Instruction for Colorado in the 1878 election. His opponent was the incumbent, Republican J. C. Shattuck, who had been elected in 1876 as the first to hold the position.[197] Goldrick "ran far ahead of his ticket throughout the State."[198] Though he did not win, his friends thought he made a good showing for the Democrats. "The party was in a great minority but the professor ran far ahead of the balance of the ticket. In this matter he was wont to take some justifiable pride."[199]

In 1879 the professor had an opportunity to reap a sizable amount of cash from an investment. He was offered $20,000 to bond a mine in which he had an interest, near Leadville. According to a piece in the *Rocky Mountain News*, he turned down the offer.[200] This contrasts with a record in the digital files of the Colorado School of Mines, which states that in 1879, Professor Goldrick bonded a mine near Leadville for $100,000.[201] No record could be found that a mining interest belonging to him generated such a windfall. If Goldrick had reaped a sum of that size, it would have surely been mentioned in his brother's diary. There is no mention of this in the Goldrick papers, nor did the professor's assets later reflect cash holdings. His estate papers indicated that at the time of his death he still owned some interest of insignificant value in one mine.[202]

Though no one would ever replace Edith, after a time the professor began to escort ladies to balls and other social functions. On one such occasion, he was dressed in his formal attire to attend a charity ball and en route to pick up a lady friend, when his carriage lost a wheel. The driver stepped down to replace it, spooked the horses, and the animals took off at a gallop, banging the hack against lampposts and curbs, with Goldrick inside yelling, "Murder!"

His peers at the *Rocky Mountain News* delighted in entertaining their readers the next morning with the story of Professor Goldrick's "great adventure."

> Goldrick said that the inside of the hack was as dark as the place not believed in by Bob Ingersoll. "A man could go through a thousand battles and not stand as good a show of getting killed as I did. And still the bloody horses went on. The ride occupied just thirty-five minutes by my watch. I thought over everything

I had ever done and a good many things I never did do. The hack was gradually being smashed into smithereens. Finally the horses dashed into a d - - d brick pile, or something, and I hollered out to somebody to bring an axe and smash the d - - d thing open so I could get out. At last an old woman came out and smashed the thing. I got out, the most frightened man that ever lived in Denver. D - - d the hack, d - - d the horses, d - - d the idiotic driver, and d - - d the whole d - - d outfit. After getting out of this scrape I got into another. I went after me girl and went to the Charity Ball, and it was just like a Sunday school. Everybody was too high-toned and precise to have a good time. Altogether, last evening was a failure with me."[203]

Though the professor could speak eloquently when required, he could also curse profusely when the occasion warranted it and when ladies were not present. Some think that the Latin he bellowed at the oxen on his arrival at the camps was "on the off side."[204] Even so, he understood and appreciated the refinement of life, and had he wished to do so, could have mingled with any level of society.[205] As he approached the early 1880s, he had less inclination to mingle. His friends remained the same ones from the beginning—his fellow Fifty-niners and his journalist peers. He seemed to gradually withdraw somewhat from the mainstream of the city's social whirl, spending more time in the saloons.[206]

Two of his brothers had died at young ages from the damages of alcohol. His father had warned him that alcoholism was inherent in both sides of his family and that drink could kill him.[207] Drink did not kill him. After an evening out, he developed a chill and fever that turned into pneumonia. Too weak to call for help, he lay ill in his room for two days until his friends came looking for him. They immediately called the doctor and gathered beside his bed to keep a vigil with their colleague and friend.[208]

William ended 1882 by writing in his diary on New Year's Eve.

"This year I have lost my brother, Owen, by death, how sad it made me but it is the inevitable. I prayed for him daily. O I hope he cast himself on the Redeemer of the Whole World and received mercy and forgiveness. None but James is now living and he an old man. . . . My children are kind enough to me but O if they served God how glorious it would be. . . . My wife and daughter at home are all that could be wanted as to being careful and kind to me. . . . My sister is in Sligo. She is not well balanced in her mind but may God keep her and provide for her. James and I sent a little to her this Christmas but she has poor judgment in anything and everything. And now, O Lord, I end this year and begin the next with consecrating all I have and am to God and His Cause."[209]

Four years later, on January 1, 1886, William wrote his last entry in his diary. Still worried about the spiritual life of his children and his church, he wrote, "O how Methodism is retrogressing. Its zeal is gone out, the principal members in other years are back-sliding." Though he had enjoyed a good marriage with Clarissa, it was his beloved Matilda who occupied his mind in his last months. "I was at Reynoldsburg on last Saturday to visit the grave of my dear Matilda. O how my heart was drawn out after her memory. . . . My family troubles me much. I have nothing to give them."

Throughout his life, William showed great courage and determination. In a biography of physicians in Delaware County, Ohio, he is described as . . .

> . . . *a man perfect in habits and was exceptionally neat in his dress, and pleasant in his manners. He was a great student, and read extensively. He was a friend to students of medicine, and very courteous to his professional brethren. He was strictly orthodox, and a firm believer in remedial agents, when properly and intelligently administered. He despised sham and quackery in the profession. He was a strict church member and attended regularly the William Street M. E.* [Methodist Episcopal] *Church.*[210]

He came to America equipped with a good mind and a fierce determination to live a righteous and useful life. He succeeded admirably, and yet he spent many hours in fruitless worry. Methodism managed to survive, and his descendants apparently did quite well for themselves. James and Owen left no children. William's progeny went on to become scholars, many of whom are distinguished educators. They are spread around the continental United States and in Hawaii, Australia, and China. One of William's great-great-great-grandsons, Robert Johnson, served as director of music programs for the Denver Public Schools, and for many years, served as organist for the St. Thomas Episcopal Church in Denver. Another of William's descendants is a scholar whose propensity for languages follows the family lineage from the patriarch back in Ireland. Matthew Goldrick, a PhD in linguistics, teaches and does research at Northwestern University and is a descendant of Owen Scott Goldrick, the language interpreter and family patriarch who sent his sons to America back in the mid-1800s.[211]

James had a career that included many years of teaching, then serving as principal of schools in Wellsburg, Virginia (now West Virginia); Steubenville, Ohio; Baltimore, Ohio; Columbus, Ohio; and Pickaway County in Ohio.[212] Throughout his life, he nurtured his family and solved their myriad problems. His love of his family is evidenced by the support he gave them and by his careful saving of the family letters.

Owen left a written account of Colorado's first school, a historical sketch of early Denver, a flood story that will be read for many generations, and a school that carries his name. Through his newspaper work, he bequeathed writings that tell the story of the development of early Colorado. He also left unanswered questions. Did he lie about being a college graduate? Why do twentieth and twenty-first-century authors write false things about him? Are the thousands upon thousands of words he left us a worthy legacy?

Chapter 10

A Worthy Legacy?

When he was writing as the Observer for the *Missouri Democrat*, Professor Goldrick called himself a Penny-a-Liner, and it has been said that he gave more to his *Herald* than it gave to him. His writing has been described as alternately boring, extravagantly wordy, lyrical, and brilliant.

In a book called *Denver!* (1972), the authors could not understand how Goldrick, author of the "dullest column in the history of the *Rocky Mountain News*," could get owners-editors William Byers and John Dailey to approve his copy.[213]

Goldrick's contemporary, Frank Hall, in his *History of the State of Colorado* (1891), declared that Goldrick's travel pieces were "of a breezy, descriptive order, relating to humorous incidents for the day, but leaving no lasting impression."[214] Eight years later, in an odd reversal of that critique, Hall wrote:

> *Soon after his* [Goldrick's] *advent Mr. Byers appointed him local editor of the* News. *While in this capacity he traveled all over Colorado, extending his trips to New Mexico, Utah, Arizona and penetrating certain of the border states of Old Mexico, whence he wrote many sparkling descriptive letters to the paper. In style and finish, brightened by exquisite touches of humor, these communications have not been excelled by any press writer of later times.*[215]

The travel letters that Hall referred to emanated from the professor's trip from Denver to Santa Fe in 1864, while he was reporting for the *Rocky Mountain News*. Historian Janet Lecompte analyzed these travel pieces in a 1996 *Journal of the Southwest* article. She pointed out that though the professor's writing was filled with "pointless metaphors and redundancies" and other outdated rhetoric, Goldrick managed to capture a picture of areas that were changing rapidly. She noted that "his glimpse of people and their opinions become increasingly precious."[216]

A *New York Courier* reporter in 1864 wrote that Goldrick possessed the "Himalaya of Style," teasingly commenting on the professor's high-flying rhetoric, and quoting his description of waking up at one of his traveling spots and catching the stagecoach:

> *T'was Wednesday morning. The steam whistle of Moyn & Rico's mill and the shrill short sound of the Planter's second bell burst on the circumambient air and blew the atmospheric bellows against our areolar tympanum, sounding the melodies of morn, and telling us 'twas time to desert our couch, don our unmentionables, get some spiritual and physical strength, and start per Cottrell & Co.'s swift and comfortable stage line for the South and intermediate settlements. We did so, just as Phoebus, fresh from his Atlantic bath, bolted out of his orient gate and glistened the gloomy, grey-eyed morning air with golden beams of beauty.*[217]

Though his writing style was, indeed, sometimes "Himalayan," Goldrick imparted useful information. If one wants to know what Colorado City (Colorado Springs), Pueblo, Trinidad, Fort Union, Moro, Las Vegas, or Santa Fe were like in 1864, consult Goldrick's prolific travel writing during that period.[218] His peers at the *Rocky Mountain News* believed that no one knew more about this western country than Goldrick.[219] He filled the pages of the *News* and later, his *Rocky Mountain Herald*, with facts about the region that can be useful to scholars today.

Goldrick's writing was well received in his day. The wild popularity of his Observer articles is an example. His travel pieces were apparently appealing to subscribers who had limited access to reading material and who enjoyed learning about places that were new to them. If anyone at the *News* thought that the professor's writing was over the top, no one stepped in to edit him. His flood story in 1864 was extravagant in its wordiness but well received and reprinted many times.

Robert Perkins, in his *First Hundred Years*, reprinted the story for his readers, saying, "His lyrical essay on the memorable flood has become the most famous news item in the annals of Denver journalism."[220]

The value of the professor's writing is underscored by an odd turn of twentieth-century fate when two beloved and respected historians inadvertently validated his ability by including several transcriptions and quotes from Goldrick's work without realizing whose words they were using.

LeRoy Hafen served as Colorado State Historian from 1924 until 1954 and also served as director of the Colorado State Museum and editor of *Colorado Magazine*. He was one of the founders of the Western History Association.[221] Hafen wrote many books individually and with his wife, Ann, also an accomplished historian. Their books have been used extensively in Colorado schools as texts and reference books. Two of the books were edited collections of letters and reports that Pike's Peakers had sent back East and that were subsequently published in eastern newspapers.

The painstaking process of collecting these letters and reports from old newspapers started in the 1920s when Elmer R. Burkey of the Colorado Historical Society began the careful process of reviewing and copying articles. This effort was continued by Dr. and Mrs. James F. Willard of the University of Colorado. The combined work of these historians created an impressive collection of rich material that Hafen saw as a boon to historians and the general public. If select letters were published in book form, they would give accounts from a variety of pioneers and illuminate the world of the Fifty-eighters and Fifty-niners. The book would create a source of information that would not otherwise be seen.[222]

Hafen edited the first collection that covered materials from 1858 through June 1859. Titled *Colorado Gold Rush: Contemporary Letters and Reports*, it was published in 1941. For the second collection of the reports and letters, LeRoy and Ann Hafen selected letters from June through December of 1859. They included several letters from the Wildman family written by Thomas Wildman, his wife, and his brother.

This book of Wildman letters, combined with select letters and reports, was published in 1961 as part of a Far West historical series and titled *Reports from Colorado: The Wildman Letters 1859–65, and Other Related Letters and Newspaper Reports, 1859*.

From the large collection of letters published in eastern newspapers, the Hafens chose several from the *Missouri Democrat*. Two of them were unsigned, and a third was signed "K." As a footnote for one of these unsigned letters, the Hafens wrote, "Published in the *Missouri Democrat*, St. Louis, June 6, 1859. The correspondent has not been positively identified."[223] The Hafens included several additional letters from a series that began in the *Democrat* on November 22, 1859.[224] On that date, the paper announced a new Pike's Peak correspondent:

> *On our first page today, will be found a long and interesting letter from Auraria and Denver City. This is the first of a series received from a very reliable and competent correspondent, whom we have engaged to write us during the coming winter.*

The first letter in the series began:

> *In compliance with your liberal proposition, I propose to forward to your paper, per every express mail, a comprehensive and truthful summary of all the general and particular news and items of interest afloat throughout this whole important region, during the ensuing season . . . everything that may appear to my judgment to prove of interest and satisfaction to the thousands*

and thousands in your neighboring sections who contemplate emigrating here in the spring, as well as for the benefit of the general readers at home. [225]

The letter went on to tell of the efforts of the territorial legislature, news about businesses, home building, theater performances at the Apollo Hall, and the story of a Mr. Burrows who went back to the states with fifty pounds of gold and returned to the camps claiming that he turned it into coin at the Philadelphia Mint for sixteen to eighteen dollars an ounce, including all the cleanings. This first letter and further letters in the series were signed "Observer."

Nowhere in the Hafens' *Reports from Colorado*, either in a footnote or elsewhere, was the Observer identified. On page 266 of their book, the Hafens excerpted a letter from Augustus Wildman in which the young pioneer told his parents about the McClure-Goldrick incident. The Hafens footnoted this entry, saying that Goldrick was Colorado's first schoolteacher and was a journalist for eastern newspapers. In one of the Observer letters included in the Hafens' book, the Observer disguised his identity when mentioning the schoolteacher. He pretended not to know how to spell the name, referring to the schoolteacher as "G—." The Hafens footnoted the entry, explaining that "G—" referred to O. J. Goldrick, Colorado's first schoolteacher. [226]

Though the *Democrat* also printed letters written by others, the Observer letters were introduced with a flourish by the paper and printed in a series from November 22, 1859, to October 11, 1860. Each was signed "Observer." Each had Goldrick's characteristic flare and style. The series included thirty-four letters. Thirty-one of these popular letters were printed on the front page. [227]

In a letter published in the *Missouri Democrat* on December 28, 1859, the Observer encouraged emigrants to bring their families:

There are thousands of acres of good land yet unclaimed, lying along our streams and parks, and they only await the magic touch of the persevering farmer to spring into life and yield abundantly the necessaries and luxuries of life. . . . If you have a wife and family, bring them also along with you, your housekeeping furniture, your clothing and your library. You will find before you and them a well-disposed refined community, where they enjoy all the comforts of a quiet home or the pleasures of the social circle; or the advantages of good schools and the privileges of churches as much if not more perhaps, than the region which you have left.

This was written in a time when Goldrick had located a better school cabin with a door and glazed windows. He knew that his school would be ready in improved quarters in time for the spring migration. In the Hafens' *Reports from Colorado* this letter was reproduced along with a footnote. "This letter may or may not have affected the emigration; but it cannot be denied that more families came in 1860 and more persons with the intention of making permanent homes in the new country."[228]

In 1976, beloved historian Robert Athearn published *The Coloradans*. Author of numerous western histories, Athearn has been called a foremost historian of Colorado and the American West. In this Colorado centennial history, he included the story of Goldrick's grand entrance into the Cherry Creek settlements in the summer of 1859. Then, in order to tell the early Colorado story, he used the Hafens' *Reports from Colorado* as it was meant to be used—as a source for firsthand accounts. By tracing Athearn's footnotes to their sources in the Hafens' book, one finds that eighteen of the footnotes lead to the writings of the Observer. Athearn used six direct quotes and the rest, indirect quotes. Not only did he not identify the Observer as Goldrick, Athearn referred to the Observer as a miner in three of the excerpts.[229]

On page 37 of his book, Athearn quoted from the Observer's comments reprinted in the Hafens' book. Athearn noted that a young miner, after going to a dance, was impressed with "these Denver adorables" with "their dainty mouths, their delicately arched brows, their clouds of silken curls and eyes" which made him "dream of intangible visions of love and happiness in the future . . ."

The person writing about the dainty mouths and intangible dreams was not a miner. He was Professor Goldrick, writing as the Observer. Athearn used the Hafens' edited *Reports from Colorado* that did not include the rest of that Observer article. By going to the original *Missouri Democrat*, one sees that the Observer went on to say:

> *I have touched upon low-necked dresses, and I am going to stand up for them, too! "What is beauty if it be not seen— Or what isn't seen, if not admired?" . . . single and widowed gents, who are pining for wives to adorn their cabins, share their claims, and weigh their dust . . . want damsels to satisfy the demand of the market, and are willing to go a big figure on a superfine article. But the latter must be of admirable texture and warranted "fast color" and not, like our Bourbon whiskey stock, "mixed or adulterated." . . . Now, then fair readers, I say come on to Pike's Peak. . . . We have thousands of fine young men and also young widowers who were "unfortunate" in their "first loves," who will receive you with outspread arms. . . . If so what a premium on hoops there will be here and how crinoline will go up—commercially speaking.*[230]

One can understand why the professor, teaching school and organizing a Sunday school at the time, preferred to remain anonymous. Though he sought anonymity in 1859 and 1860, he would no doubt have been delighted to know that two of Colorado's respected historians selected material from his writing out of hundreds of original letters and reports. Like being drawn to writings of a close friend, but without knowing him to be the author, the Hafens and Athearn were attracted to the vitality produced by the Observer's pen.

By choosing to use the Observer's words, Ann and LeRoy Hafen and Robert Athearn captured the firsthand views of a clever, articulate Fifty-niner, and at the same time, bestowed on Colorado's first schoolteacher a status that he craved—that of historian.[231] Athearn's centennial history was published one hundred years after the professor stood before the large crowd in the grove in Denver delivering his "Historical Sketch of Denver, Colorado" address in celebration of Colorado becoming a state.

A tribute to Goldrick in the *Denver Tribune*, November 27, 1882, said:

> *In 1860, when the Professor first embarked in the newspaper business, he became the regular correspondent for the St. Louis* Democrat *and wrote a famous characteristic letter to that paper describing the society of the city in his usual style, which was widely copied in all papers of the East. As a graphic descriptive writer very few could equal him.*

Goldrick was able to make a living with his active pen for twenty-two years and would have continued to do so had he not died at the age of fifty-three. Significant evidence suggests that many people enjoyed his droll wit, keen observations, and tongue-in-cheek jabs at the people and events of the day. His early travel pieces and articles for the *Rocky Mountain News*, his humorous, descriptive letters as the Observer for the *Missouri Democrat*, his vivid account of the 1864 flood of Cherry Creek, and his pages and pages of archived writing in his *Herald* leave students of history a treasure that has not yet been fully mined.

Chapter 11

The Truth about Professor Goldrick

Professor Owen Joseph Goldrick was admittedly a peculiar person. His brother William in his diary referred to him as such.[232] All who knew him declared that he was a genuine character. We may not understand exactly what these characteristics mean. What is certain is that he was well known and fondly regarded by his contemporaries throughout the Rocky Mountain region.[233] Yet in the twentieth and twenty-first centuries, authors and journalists have written stories about him that call for further clarification. Some have a thread of truth woven through them, and others are not true at all. Did Goldrick claim college degrees that he did not have? Did he die a miserable death in a lonely rented room? Did he die in abject poverty?

Modern authors sometimes seem too eager to paint the professor as a chronic alcoholic who struggled to stay in control. Most of the people who knew him did not think of him in that light. Though he struggled the last few months of his life, the body of his time in Denver was quite productive and could not have been accomplished had he been too entrapped by the need of a bottle.

Another example of a modern misconception involves the story of Goldrick leaving the *Rocky Mountain News* to follow his ambition to become an editor. One author suggested that Goldrick left the *News* because he was unappreciated by editor William Byers, and that, when he returned to Denver and started his own paper, he did so because he was "still at odds with the *News*."[234] The source for this version of Goldrick's endeavors was not provided, and the story seems at odds with what is known about Byers's continued interest in and support of the professor.

Though Byers was a strong Republican and Goldrick was a Democrat, the two men shared many of the same views. They both believed that agriculture and trade would play as significant a role in Colorado's development as mining. They also shared the view that schools, churches, and cultural institutions were vital in the development of their state. As has been stated, Byers promoted Goldrick to associate editor, presented him with a gold pen when the professor left his employ, and published his articles long after the professor left the *News*. Byers, of all people, would have understood the ambition of a capable journalist—ambition to edit his own newspaper. Byers served as a pallbearer at Goldrick's funeral.

Confusing stories about Goldrick's education abound. Authors have written that he "claimed" to have college degrees from Trinity College in Dublin and from Columbia College, now Columbia University.[235]

Was the professor a con man? Not likely. Extensive reading of his writing revealed no evidence that he claimed college degrees. Some, however, might make a good argument that he claimed them by default—by not denying having them. Perhaps he hinted at having such schooling. If he did, then why didn't the booster newspaper mention these degrees when they touted Goldrick and his school?

When Goldrick arrived at the Cherry Creek settlements, he did not seek the honorary title of professor. The townsfolk bestowed it on him. His contemporary, Jerome Smiley, wrote that "the people, who were fond of bestowing titles . . . soon begin [sic] calling him 'Professor,' a distinction to which he made no claim, himself."[236] Archival newspapers of the day may have gems hidden about the professor that wait to be discovered, but many hours of microfilm review failed to show that Goldrick stated that he was a college man.

A review of the era's writing suggests that naming the universities that Goldrick attended and the degrees he acquired did not surface until late in his life. In W. B. Vickers's *History of the City of Denver* (1880) published two years before Goldrick's death, Vickers wrote that Goldrick "was educated in the University of Dublin, and afterward in Columbia College, New York." Vickers also wrote that Goldrick "has little regard for the conventionalities of society, and heartily detests sham and hypocrisy in all its forms."[237] It is possible that an offhand remark about his education was misinterpreted. By the time Vickers's exaggerated account of Goldrick's education appeared in print, the professor may have felt that it was embarrassingly late to publicly state that he was not a college man. Two or three of his obituaries mention the degrees, so presumably some journalists thought that they were real.[238] Did these newspaper men get their information from Vickers's then-recently published book? When writing Goldrick's obituary, one of the writers lifted a full and exact sentence from the book.[239] One wonders if any of his peers ever asked Goldrick about his education, or just assumed what Vickers wrote was correct.

A fellow journalist who knew Goldrick for twenty years wrote, "He was a thorough hater of shams and despised alike a hypocrite or deadbeat."[240] It seems quite unusual that a man remembered in those terms would deliberately lie about his schooling.

Judge Marshall Silverthorne, a Fifty-niner who lived in Summit County, had known the professor from their days back in Pennsylvania and later "in the valley and always maintained a close and warm friendship."[241] The judge held Goldrick in high regard. Would Goldrick have tried to con the citizens of Colorado with Judge Silverthorne there as a fellow pioneer?

After Goldrick's death, stories began to emerge in print describing him and his education. Authors stated that he arrived in Colorado with a degree from Columbia in his pocket.[242] Untrue. Most of the articles written after his death that told of his entrance into Auraria also told of his college education. Some said he was educated in Dublin, and

99

others specified that it was Trinity College in Dublin. Yet others added the second degree from Columbia College. Long after Goldrick's death, Frank Hall, who knew Goldrick well enough to be a pallbearer at his funeral, wrote that the professor had been educated for the priesthood in Dublin before running away and coming to America.[243] One wonders where Hall heard such a falsehood.

Inexplicably, in the 1920s, long after the professor's death, a master of arts degree from Columbia was added, and continued to be reported.[244] Authors overlooked research by Harry M. Barrett, director of the College of Education at the University of Colorado, who wrote in 1935 that neither Trinity College in Dublin nor Columbia University could find Goldrick listed as a former student. These findings were subsequently confirmed by a Goldrick family member, and again, by the author.[245] Journalists continued to write about his elite college degrees. Robert Perkins's *The First Hundred Years: An Informal History of Denver and the Rocky Mountain News* and Nolie Mumey's Goldrick biography were published in the same year (1959). Mumey gave Goldrick the undergraduate degree from Trinity College plus the ". . . M.A. degree from Columbia University in New York." Perkins stated that the degrees did not exist.[246] Authors began to assume and write that Goldrick "claimed" these degrees.

If Goldrick was intent on falsely enhancing his résumé, he missed several opportunities to do so. In the flyer produced in 1848 in Pennsylvania to promote their school, brother James made no mention of his education or Owen's.[247] The professor's Union School announcement said nothing about his education.[248] When the *News* encouraged school attendance in 1859 and 1860, the paper boasted about Goldrick's ability to teach and administer effective discipline, but did not mention where he was educated.[249] In the 1870s Goldrick sought the position of state superintendent of education and wrote a piece in his *Herald* that told of his strong belief in and lifetime support of public education for all races and creeds.[250] When presenting his credentials, he made no mention of his education.

In a strong endorsement of Goldrick as the 1878 candidate for state education superintendent, the *Colorado Transcript* called him a "Colorado Thoroughbred." The paper pointed out that he was an old and experienced teacher, the teacher of Colorado's first school and first Sabbath school, the founder of free schools in the New West, the first organizer of school districts in Denver, and the first school superintendent elected in Arapahoe County, the "first man who had the pluck to plant education in the heart of the 'American Desert,' and thus timely aided in the first settlement and the first civilization of what is now the great Centennial State." The endorsement made no mention of Goldrick's education.[251]

Owen and his brothers, William and James, had solid educational backgrounds when they arrived in America. They wrote well and had good vocabularies. All three had no trouble getting jobs and gaining certification as teachers. William was able to qualify for and handle medical studies with success. From their letters, one senses that the other brothers in the family did not have such good training. It is possible that the two oldest had advantages that the others did not have due to the financial problems that came to Ireland. Then, baby Owen came along. The youngest, and very bright, perhaps he got special attention from his father and his two oldest brothers. He had a quick mind, thirsty for knowledge. James had several younger brothers. He must have had a good reason to choose Owen to bring to America.[252]

Owen's love of books is evident in his letters. A few months after his arrival at Cherry Creek, he presented the *Rocky Mountain News* office with a geography book to help writers and editors to be accurate.[253]

Perhaps toward the end of his life, the professor allowed the stories to flourish but was too smart to put them in print himself. Then again, he may have been immune or oblivious to what people said about him. What is known is that he was an enigma to his peers. When he died, his closest associates did not know his full name and thus used merely the initials "O. J." on his tombstone. He was Irish, so they assumed he was Catholic. The date of birth on his tombstone is off by four years.

The journalist who wrote that "while everybody seemed to know him, no one knew him well enough to write a true history of his life"[254] was correct. It was as though a vacuum created by lack of knowledge of the professor's true story was filled with the imaginings of others.

Possibly, further information will emerge from something missed in Goldrick's writing contained in archival newspapers. Perhaps a Goldrick family member has an enlightening old letter not yet read by historians. Until and unless such information comes to light, Goldrick's intent regarding his academic résumé will remain an enigma that matches the man.

What about repeated statements that he was dissipated and died a miserable death in a lonely rented room?[255] Ample evidence suggests that Goldrick was a drinking man. The story most often repeated of his drinking was told by S. T. Sopris, who worked with Goldrick at the *News* in the early days of the paper. He wrote:

> *While on the* News, *Goldrick became sadly dissipated, seldom going to bed sober, or for that matter, seldom "hitting the hay" twice in the same room. He was known by everyone, and usually had no trouble in finding shelter any hour of the night. It became the regular thing in the office, when the city editor failed to show up by noon, for the boss to say "who will go and find Goldrick?" The* News *went to press at five o'clock, and Goldrick could output enough "copy" to fill his page in two or three hours, if he could be found in time.*[256]

In an article in *Colorado Magazine* in 1929, Levette Jay Davidson, professor of American literature at the University of Colorado, quoted the Sopris article, and then added that Sopris had "painted with relish what is probably an exaggerated picture of Goldrick's Bohemian way of life at this period." Davidson continued:

> *One of Goldrick's newspaper assignments was to meet the overland stage coaches upon their arrival in Denver and to get*

the latest news of the outside world, for the telegraph did not reach Denver until October, 1863. Frank A. Root, who served as one of the guards on the several trips of the overland mail coach, has left us a description of the arrival of the Atchison stage in Denver on Sunday, January 29, 1863, after six days on the road. After noting the crowd of between five hundred and a thousand people gathered at the Planter's House to greet the stage and to talk over the news brought by messenger and passengers, Root continues: "As soon as I had checked off my 'run' at the office, Prof. O. J. Goldrick, Denver's noted pioneer newspaper reporter, was the first stranger to greet me in search of news along the overland line." [257]

Goldrick was a working journalist who drank to excess on occasions. The scene Sopris described surely happened at times. Another fellow journalist who knew him well stated that Goldrick "was at periods reckless and wild—wine and women being his besetting sins." The article went on to say that Goldrick was one of the brightest journalists of the West.[258] In spite of these periodic bouts of indiscretion on Goldrick's part, it seems doubtful that an enterprising businessman like W. N. Byers, Goldrick's boss at the time, would have put up with drunken behavior on a steady basis or that he would appoint a person with irresponsible habits as managing editor and send him all over the countryside as a goodwill ambassador for the paper—to encourage ads and subscriptions. Would Byers have promoted—from managing editor to associate editor as he did in 1864—a man who had to be dragged each day from the saloons?[259]

During his travels for the *News*, and then later for his own newspapers, Goldrick's presence generated comments that indicate that fellow journalists not only liked him but had confidence in his ability. Once people got used to his straightforward manner, they seemed to be drawn to him. It is said that he had no enemies, and his friends were always glad to see him. Though he had a stern outward countenance in his formal clothing, his quick wit dissolved any controversy into laughter. His fellow journalists often wrote about him.

When he returned to Denver after the sojourn in Utah, the *Rocky Mountain News* wrote, "Our 'illustrious predecessor,' O. J. Goldrick, Esq., at present one of the editors of the *Vedette* of Salt Lake arrived here yesterday on a short business visit. We are glad to shake his Irish fist once again."[260]

The *Colorado Transcript* wrote, "The gay and gallant Celt, O. J. Goldrick, of the *Times* was in town last week. Goldrick is a good boy, and can scribble a telling newspaper item equal to the best, and we are always glad to see him."[261]

When Goldrick started his own *Rocky Mountain Herald*, his effort was soundly endorsed by other editors.[262] A Cheyenne paper wrote, "The *Herald* is destined to rank among the first-class journals of the Rocky Mountain country. In typographical appearance it is a perfect model."[263]

A reminiscence piece written in 1883 described Goldrick. "In conversation he was jovial, quick to repartee, and with his pen could polish a sentence as none other could. A little eccentric—always original—and at times he was eloquently brilliant."[264]

Though it may have been "painted with relish what is probably an exaggerated story," as Davidson said, Sopris's quotation about Goldrick's excessive drinking seems to have influenced modern writers of the professor's story. One seldom sees the quotation by the driver of the stage who describes Goldrick as a hardworking journalist.

Sopris had more to say about Goldrick. He stated that Goldrick was "a prominent figure in the social and business world of Denver." He went on to say:

> *Going to Chicago to secure materials for the* Herald, *he met a middle-aged widow, a fine woman, and after a brief acquaintance, they were married, and now comes the surprising part of the story. From the time he met her until after her death,*

five or more years, Goldrick did not touch or taste liquor, and was one of the best behaved and best dressed men in Denver. It is one instance where a woman reformed a man by marrying him. As I remember it, he drank more or less after her death, and did not long survive her.[265]

The Sopris account of Goldrick's drinking made it appear that, except for the few years he was married, he was seldom sober. This was underscored in a modern book, *The '59ers*. This popular book telling of Denver's first three rowdy years went through three printings and can be found in many homes and libraries. It is a rollicking account that is fun to read. After telling about some incidents in Goldrick's life, the authors summed up the professor's story by saying that the achievements of this talented "teacher, journalist, and civic leader" were remarkable in that they were accomplished during his "brief periods of sobriety."[266] Again, Goldrick was depicted as seldom being sober.

It seems unbelievable that Professor Goldrick had the support of parents who allowed him to teach their children; gained significant promotions at the *News*; was selected as superintendent of the Arapahoe County schools; ran his own newspaper almost single-handedly for fifteen years; garnered the support of advertisers, subscribers, and fellow journalists; was repeatedly asked to give speeches before large crowds, including a sketch of Denver's history at the statehood celebration; attracted and married an intelligent and cultured widow; and gained great support throughout the state in his run for state education superintendent—unbelievable that he did all of this and more while in a state of inebriation with "brief periods of sobriety."

Even Goldrick's flood story, widely read throughout the country and reprinted often, has been tainted by literary license at the professor's expense. In a feature article telling about Goldrick's historic story, one modern *Rocky Mountain News* journalist wrote, "No sir, they don't have that kind of reporting nowadays—and they don't make the kind of whisky that produced the Professor's literature."[267] The clear implication is that Goldrick's ability to write a good story was fueled by alcohol. A serious reader of the professor's writing knows that his flowing and flowery writing style was characteristic of the work that earned him a living for over two decades.

A careful study of documented history tells us that Goldrick lived a productive and useful life in spite of bouts of inebriation. His fellow pioneers apparently accepted this about him and continued to support his efforts. His friends were also aware that, toward the end of his life, he began to lose ground.

At the time of his death, evidence of his decline during the last year was revealed, but it is important that we do not measure his twenty-three-year career in Denver by his final weeks.

One obituary stated, "They are around the bier of one who had braved the dangers of the frontier with them, one who had drifted apart from the more conventional current which they had followed . . . will always hold a warm place in their hearts."[268]

A journalist peer at the *Denver Tribune* added insight into Goldrick's last year. "Some five years since, Professor Goldrick was married to a very estimable lady from Chicago, but his married life with her was of short duration. . . . After her death he seemed a changed man, and now that he is dead his many warm friends can account for his seemingly strange actions."[269]

From these clues, there is a sense that the professor was not able to follow his dear Edith's advice. Goldrick's tender tribute to her at the time of her death in 1877 was uncharacteristically open and revealing. He shared with his *Herald* readers that on her deathbed, Edith admonished him to take care of himself and his business and to live the life of a gentleman. Though the professor gave up drinking completely during his marriage, his wife apparently knew of his weaknesses and warned him against them. Goldrick was a solitary soul with many friends, and yet, there was no one in whom he confided—no one except Edith.[270] It is possible that the publicly flamboyant but emotionally reclusive man found, for the first and only time in his life, a true soul mate in Edith. After her death, he apparently gradually slipped into a less healthy lifestyle, finding conversation and companionship in the saloons.

The repeated statements that he died a miserable death in a lonely rented room elicit a tragic image of a tragic man. This account is not supported because it does not match the records preserved in every major newspaper in Colorado and the Rocky Mountain area.

Yes, the professor lived in a rented room in an inexpensive hotel conveniently located in the block near to his *Herald* office. Though it was on the notorious Holladay Street that housed local prostitutes, Goldrick's hotel was on the respectable end of the street in the business section in the Tappan Block and near the City National Bank.[271] Living in a rented room was not a sad or unusual arrangement in the early 1880s for a working widower who ate his meals at a boardinghouse or café. Denver's new-rich silver moguls may have looked upon this arrangement with disdain, but it suited the professor just fine. It was a comfortable enough room close to his place of business and in a respectable business district.

From his estate records we know what his room was like. All furnishings in the room belonged to him. His bedstead, wardrobe, and center table were made of black walnut. He owned another pine table, a washstand with a bowl and water pitcher, one Hitchcock lamp and a second lamp, a book rack with twenty-five books, a folding recliner, an easy chair, a whatnot shelf, a traveling case, five pictures, twenty yards of carpet, three rugs, mattresses, quilts, clothes, personal belongings, and a *Webster's Dictionary.*[272]

Death by pneumonia was not uncommon in that era. Excerpts from news accounts at the time of his death tell us that the professor was supported and surrounded by his friends, who did everything possible to nurture him and make him comfortable.

The professor's illness came upon him suddenly. He probably took to his bed thinking the ague would pass and that he would be better in the morning. He got worse. When his colleagues found him in severe distress in his room, they moved him to a clean, fresh room in the hotel. The people who were there with Goldrick during his final days can tell the story accurately.

The day following his death, the *Denver Tribune* stated:

> *Last Monday he was taken sick while engaged in writing in his room in the Tappan block, corner of Fifteenth and Holladay streets, and two days he lay there uncared for . . . everything was done for him that was possible. Dr. Steel was called, and after making a thorough examination of his disease at once pronounced it fatal. . . . Yesterday when it was known that Professor Goldrick was sick and fears were entertained for his recovery, his numerous friends called to pay their respects and to see if there was something they could do for him.*[273]

The *Denver Republican* remarked that Goldrick's characteristic sense of humor never left him.

> *Even on his death bed his manner of jest never failed him. Said he, but a few hours before "passing over the range"—"Bring me a barber, that I may make a presentable appearance. No pig scraper, but an artist—one who can hold his razor and his tongue at the same time."*[274]

The *Denver Tribune* described how his friends administered to his needs:

> *Late last Saturday, when it was thought by his friends that his death was a matter of only a few short hours, Wolfe Londoner spoke to him about having a minister call on him to offer a few words in his dying moments, which seemed to please him and at once sent a messenger for Bishop Machebeuf,*[275] *who soon was there ready to talk with him, but the professor refused, and wished for some orthodox minister, and requested that Rev. Dr. Jeffery be called. The request was soon complied with, and in*

his dying hours the doctor administered to his wants. When the doctor had concluded his prayer for the recovery of the dying man, the professor, with his feeble voice, thanked him and said that he was willing to die.[276]

John Riethmann, a friend always ready to help him, stated:

He seemed to appreciate that he was approaching the end, and he said to me, "John, I'll die like a gentleman; you'll hear no death rattle from me." Nor did I. He soon passed on, and with him was buried one of the most interesting and eccentric men connected with our frontier history.[277]

The professor died a few minutes before midnight. Journalist Halsey Rhoads was with him at the end, along with the nurse attendant.[278]

The Association of Colorado Pioneers appointed Wolfe Londoner, W. N. Byers, and Judge Jacob Downing to see to it that their old colleague's affairs were properly addressed.[279] It was probably these friends who selected a fine casket with a brass plate. The Denver Press Club provided a plot at Riverside Cemetery.[280] The members of the pioneer association attended the funeral as a group, wearing their badges and crape. Each daily newspaper provided a carriage for editors and reporters. The artillery company supplied an honor guard. To accommodate the large crowd, undertaker McGovern held the service in a vacant building across from the funeral home.[281]

"Miserable death in a lonely rented room" is surely an inaccurate description of the events so carefully recorded by Goldrick's colleagues. Though Professor Goldrick lost ground in his life and his health after the death of his wife, he was ever a ladies' man. When describing the funeral, the *Rocky Mountain News* reported, "A bouquet of immortelles had been placed upon the case [casket] by a lady friend. At the grave, just before the body was interred, undertaker McGovern removed this bouquet from the coffin, but the lady gently put it back again. This was one of the most touching incidents of the funeral."[282] Goldrick lonely?

It appears not.

A frequent comment by modern authors states that Goldrick was penniless when he died. It is accurate to say that Goldrick died with no money in the bank. This statement, however, does not fully explain his actual state of affairs. Cash played no big part in his existence. His attitude about money was "easy come, easy go." He managed to attend social events, take the ladies to balls, travel for his business, and dress well. How did he do this? He used a barter system. He was a good salesman and exchanged advertisements in his paper for goods and services that he needed. As one of his fellow journalists put it, he ran a newspaper that "he contrived to make him a living by a tact which was all his own, and which was as unique as his own character."[283]

It was not unusual for nineteenth-century editors to allow a business to provide items or services that were being advertised in exchange for ad space in the newspaper. Goldrick spent cash when he had it. His credit was good enough so that he could borrow small sums to tide him over when the cash flow at his paper was slow.

An unkind and unsigned letter to the *Springfield Republican* in Springfield, Massachusetts, revealed Goldrick's technique.

> *There is one picturesque newspaper genius in Denver whose image time will never fade. He is the editor of the* Rocky Mountain Herald. *His name is Goldrick. One of the traditions of Denver (a fact, too) is that he crossed the plains in 1859 in a tall hat, lavender kid gloves and a suit of broadcloth. This dress he has never deviated from. He does no work on his paper. He gets the outside printed in Chicago, has an exchange editor to fill up the inside, and the business men give him "ads" and pay for them with the necessities and luxuries of life. For example, the tailors advertise extensively and Goldrick dresses prodigiously. The livery men occupy a column, and Goldrick drives fast horses on a numerous scale, so to speak. This paper doesn't circulate, and there's the rub. He hasn't much ready money.*

His impecuniousness is history. How is this for a feature in the problem of life. A man with no money leading a luxurious life without running into debt, borrowing or living on friends![284]

The author of this letter was not accurate when he said that Goldrick did no writing for his paper. The professor filled the pages with his thoughts on all manner of subjects. However, the writer was correct in figuring out how Goldrick lived well without much cash. The phrase "this paper doesn't circulate" probably means that the *Herald* in print could not be used for circulating cash, yet it provided for the professor's needs.

His method of barter also allowed the professor to help his family. Eight days before his death and two days before his illness came upon him, he wrote a loving letter to his fifteen-year-old great-niece, Lizzie, in Ohio. One can tell that Goldrick had no idea that death was imminent.[285]

Dear Lizzie,
Denver, Colorado, November 17, '82

By the time you get this note, you will get a first class sewing machine, with all the latest improvements per express from the N.Y. manufacturers. This enclosed (remarks portion) is a description. Yet, if you don't want it, you can loan it to your mother or your "Grandma."

I will, in a few days or so, have a new and enlarged edition of Webster's Unabridged Dictionary for you to keep & consult occasionally—or, if you don't want it, you can easily have someone sell it for you in Delaware for $10 or $12 (the latter is the publisher's price).

I have an amt. of $30 due me by this Phila dry goods from whose card I enclose and I've sent to them for their illustrated price catalogue of hats, dress articles—which I will mail to you, soon, for you to select such articles you may think suitable and *for the above amount—and send the order to me, to get for you.*

Tell your "Grandma" that this tea co. whose card I enclosed owes me $20 worth of their teas and if she could use that kind there, I will direct them to express it to her.

Lizzie, I am advertising for an organ manufacturer who will owe me a $90 organ next summer, which I will have sent from his manufactory for you. When you receive the sewing machine at place inform me, by mail—and oblige.

Yours Truly
O. J. Goldrick

Lizzie's mother was the professor's niece, Susan Goldrick Chapman Robinson, the daughter of William, one who had greatly disappointed him. The stern William could not accept that Susan had eloped at age nineteen, experienced a miserable marriage, divorced Chapman, and found love and joy in her marriage to Mr. Robinson. William felt that this was an affront to his beliefs in the sanctity of marriage. During the time when Susan moved back home after her divorce, her father made her cover her glorious auburn hair with a prim white lace cap. She was not allowed to visit friends.[286]

By the time her uncle Owen was sending the sewing machine, Susan had remarried. Lizzie was a daughter from her first marriage. Susan was an expert seamstress who contributed to her family's support by making intricate christening dresses and doing fine handwork.[287] In contrast to his stern brother, the more liberal-minded Owen did not judge Susan, but wanted to help her and Lizzie. Also, Clarissa had been kind to him when he was living in Ohio. He no doubt enjoyed being able to send his sister-in-law a selection of teas.

The professor was generous to a fault. When he had money, he spent it or shared it with little regard for the days ahead. If the cash flow at the *Herald* was slow or if he had overspent, he stopped by the drugstore and borrowed ten dollars from his friend, John Riethmann. "Scarcely a day passed that he did not come into my store and generally, being broke, would ask to borrow money. . . . I invariably accommodated him and at his request would put a ticket in the drawer which he never failed to redeem."[288] This activity is no worse than present-day use of credit cards; however, Goldrick's generosity and his lifestyle left him no cash cushion. Part of his eccentricity was this impractical, easygoing way of life. Riethmann's drugstore ran ads continuously in Goldrick's paper. It is possible that the druggist received a discount on the ads for serving as the professor's creditor. Goldrick was clever at making these types of arrangements.

Records of the professor's modest philanthropies are well documented. The *Denver Tribune* told of his genuine interest in children.

> *Professor Goldrick was passionately fond of children, and many a time has been known to take a little ragged urchin into a near clothing store and after purchasing a new suit for him up and send him home rejoicing. Such little acts of kindness seemed to please him more than anything else he could do. The writer of this has known of his purchasing dozens of tickets for children and taking them to matinees, sitting in their midst while they were enjoying themselves with the play—happy in the thought that he was the means of bringing enjoyment and happiness into the lives of some poor children.*[289]

A fellow journalist who had known him for many years commented on his character:

> *Tender-hearted as a woman and as generous and free-handed as a bonanza king, though nearly always "hard-up" for money, he was a friend to the poor and needy and his deeds of charity, few of which were known to the out-side world as plenty as were the kindly words spoken by him of and to his fellow men.*[290]

The Association of Colorado Pioneers spoke of his generosity in a published tribute to him that declared that he was "a generous, warm-hearted, liberal-handed citizen, who has done much for the state."[291]

The *Denver Times* spoke of "his sympathy with the poor, and his love and kindness for little children; how he always had a kind word for them, or an apple or a piece of candy or any trifle that would make them happy."[292]

The *Denver Tribune* stated that "he was one of those peculiar men who did acts of kindness not for show but for the good they did those receiving them."[293]

When Owen was on his deathbed, he confided to his friend Wolfe Londoner that he had accumulated no cash but that his business and personal interests were solvent.[294] As it turned out, his meager estate did not quite cover his meager bills.

Goldrick's estate papers mention brothers who lived out of state. Apparently Colorado law at that time allowed the courts to settle an estate that had no will and no relatives living in Colorado. Judge B. F. Harrington appointed the manager of the mechanical department at Goldrick's *Herald*, John P. Heisler, as executor. Goldrick owned the *Herald* and its equipment and the furniture and personal items in his hotel room. He also owned one-fourth interest in the City Lode situated in the California Mining District in Lake County, Colorado, near Oro City.[295] It is unclear if this is the same mine for which the professor was offered a bond in 1879.[296]

Judge Harrington allowed a private sale of assets. It took from November of 1882 until June of 1886 to settle the modest estate. Goldrick's friends thought that his interest in the mine would be ample to cover all expenses;[297] however, its sale brought only $200 when purchased by W. R. Rust. After bills for the doctor, funeral home, accounts at stores, court costs, and a few small bills were paid, the estate lacked $241 to cover what was owed.[298] The professor would have been embarrassed to leave this earth without paying all of his bills. He was known to have a low opinion of deadbeats.

Inconsistencies in Goldrick's story abound. John Riethmann, a Fifty-eighter who operated the first drugstore in the Cherry Creek settlements and who loaned Goldrick small sums when needed, was a credible witness. In an interview with T. F. Dawson in 1922, he spoke about his old friend:

> *No man in Denver was so resplendent as he. He always wore a silk hat and a frock coat, and being tall, slender and pale, presented an appearance which commanded attention. The buttons on his coat might easily have created the impression that he was a lackey, but everybody knew that he was not, and to all old-timers these very buttons were a distinguishing mark. They were not brass, but gold—solid gold—Colorado Gold fresh from our own mines. He also wore a solitaire diamond scarf pin as big as the end of your thumb. Oh, he surely was a dresser.[299]*

Goldrick's clothes were appraised for ten dollars and sold with his other belongings at a private sale. No gold buttons or diamond stickpins were mentioned.

Owen had not heeded his father's earlier admonitions to "be just before you are generous."[300] Owen Scott knew his son well. Had Goldrick not been so generous through the years, his estate would have had the funds to "be just" and cover the small sum that was owed. Apparently his friend John Riethmann lost no money when Goldrick died. Though estate papers mentioned bills as small as two dollars, no mention was made of unpaid tickets in the drugstore drawer.

The professor's final account at the John Sinclair and Company clothing store was illuminating. An unusually large number of pairs of kid gloves had been purchased in the years prior to his death.[301]

Lizzie and her mother probably got the sewing machine that had already shipped when Goldrick wrote his final letter to his great-niece. The tea, the organ, the credit at the clothing store, and the new *Webster's Unabridged Dictionary* most likely became part of the accounts receivable and converted to cash to help keep the paper going. Estate executor John Heisler, already an employee of the *Herald*, kept the paper in publication while the estate was being settled. Halsey Rhodes, who helped with the business end of the paper and who was the last friend to be with Goldrick at his death, became the new editor.[302] The *Rocky Mountain Herald,* saved from oblivion by Goldrick, continued under various ownerships well into the twentieth century.

So, yes, it is true that Goldrick was penniless when he died. He managed to provide for himself and to help others with his lack of concern for cash and with his barter system. It is apparent that he did not think of himself as poor or as being too pinched to send generous gifts to his family. For many years, he sustained the *Herald,* and it sustained him. Modern historians and journalists who judge him as a man who died in poverty are missing a true understanding of the professor and his eccentricities. After all, he had good credit and a business that made him a living. Historians in his day had a better understanding of him. In his 1880 history of Denver, W. B. Vickers wrote that the professor "accepts the smiles and frowns of fortune with supreme indifference, openly content whether he smokes his 'dhudeen' [sic] or 50 cent cigars."[303]

Another quotation about the professor lacks documentation and paints a sad picture of him. "Professor Goldrick's roll-top desk probably more than a century old and somewhat the worse for wear where whiskey had eaten into the varnish continues its usefulness in the editorial meditations of the *Rocky Mountain Herald.*"[304]

This statement conjures an image of Goldrick sitting at his desk slopping alcohol all over his writing papers. The provenance of the desk described is that it was an old desk that was in the office of the *Herald.* There is no certain evidence that it belonged to Goldrick or that he used it or that the stains on it were made by alcohol. Goldrick's estate papers lend credence to the idea that one of the later owners of the paper brought the desk to the *Herald* office.

There were two inventories of Goldrick's personal and business belongings. One was an initial inventory, and the second was the legal inventory presented to the court. They were essentially the same in content. Neither made any mention of a rolltop desk or any other type of desk. Goldrick had a walnut table in the center of his hotel room and another "common" table at which he wrote. The *Herald* office inventory mentions no desk. These inventories are detailed lists that include such things as a looking glass, a water pitcher, two sheets, a bed spring, and so on. The *Herald* business office list gives details such as one shooting stick, one galley rack, and the like. It seems unlikely that the two inventories would have failed to mention a rolltop desk if it were in fact there.[305]

A final example of modern-day negative press about the professor states, "An effort to name a school after Denver's first school teacher failed some years ago because the 'professor' had been a drinking man."[306]

Twenty years prior to the date that this piece was published, the Owen J. Goldrick Elementary School was built and dedicated on Denver's South Zuni Street. Francis M. Bain, who served on the school board when the school was named and built, wrote in response to an inquiry, "I do not recall that there was any controversy or lengthy discussion about naming the school after Goldrick. It seemed like a thoughtful thing to do."[307] At the school's dedication, board of education member Frank Traylor told the traditional story of Goldrick's arrival in Auraria and his establishment of the first school. He followed the description of the humble log school with these comments:

It was Goldrick who led the first crusade for tax-supported public education. In 1861, he was elected Superintendent of Schools for Arapahoe County[308] and, during the two years in which he held this position, School District Number One was organized east of Cherry Creek. Number Two ran west of Cherry Creek. This was the story of O. J. Goldrick, "Professor," as the town called him. Throughout his life until his death in 1882 he worked for all good causes promoting the welfare of Denver. . . . In the hope that the citizens of today will have equal courage in promoting the welfare of children and the community, we have named this school for O. J. Goldrick.

Among the items placed in the school's cornerstone is a miniature model of Goldrick's first school, constructed in 1946 by Nancy West of Skinner Junior High School, along with a photograph of some students from that school. Essays and excerpts from plays written by students of Skinner Junior High School, Gilpin School, and Byers Junior High were included. The cornerstone also contains a book about the Denver Mint by Nolie Mumey and E. H. Gruber, a copy of Goldrick's *Historical Sketch of Denver, Colorado*, and a brief story of the professor's life.[309]

Chapter 12

Remembering the Professor

Goldrick was a man with energy, talents, flaws, and weaknesses. It was through his actions that his image of being a drinking man evolved, and by his unwillingness to talk about himself, he created an environment where fables flourished. However, embellishing his weaknesses with undocumented stories hampers the development of a balanced account of his life. The professor's record as a Colorado pioneer reveals him to be a keenly intelligent, enthusiastic promoter of his adopted home. His love of learning was contagious at a time when the raw settlements on Cherry Creek were most in need of such an influence.

He lived five years after his wife's death. During the last year of his life, he was not as active as he had been, and yet, he was still a functioning citizen. Archived newspapers tell us that during this time, he was still productive and reasonably sociable. He lived in the hotel near his office building and survived well enough on his barter system. In 1881, the year before his death, he joined the Colorado State Historical Society.[310] During this time, he was still serving on committees as a member of the Colorado Pioneers.[311] Goldrick was an active member of the long-standing Denver Press Club, a group that met informally to discuss events, play poker, and sip Taos Lightning.[312] Just four months before his death, he was welcomed into the Colorado State Press Association.[313] A short time before that, he gave a speech at a banquet at the Teller House before a large crowd of members and guests of Gilpin County's pioneers.[314] During that period he gave another speech to the pioneer ladies of Denver,[315] escorted lady friends to balls, and got his paper out on time.

An explanation of his ability to be dependable in his final year, to show up as a guest speaker, and to meet his obligations to his family and his business might be found in this note he wrote in his *Herald*:

> *General Sherman says: "I don't believe that Grant was ever drunk when there was any fighting to be done." This is a limited certificate of sobriety, but it certainly ought to go a great way. The trouble with a great many men is that they get drunk at the wrong time.*[316]

Perhaps toward the end of his life, Goldrick was able to continue to meet his responsibilities because he had learned to parse his drinking to times when sobriety was not essential. His classic description of his first school was written in 1882, the year of his death. Fortunately it was saved and made accessible in the Historical Society's *Colorado Magazine* in 1929.[317]

Throughout his adult life, his manner of dress may have given the impression of pretentiousness. People who knew him well declared that this was not his nature. Goldrick detested the pretentions of polite society and presented himself in a straightforward manner.[318] Other than his longtime custom of dressing in fine clothes, he made no attempt to impress. "He made no claims of exaltation upon his fellow man, but was content if allowed to pursue his course unmolested and to elbow his own way through the crowd."[319] With Goldrick, there was no hidden agenda. "He was eccentric, and blunt to a degree that was often surprising. He was nothing if not sincere. . . .Whatever may have been said of him, no one could ever accuse him of a selfish action or a deed that was unkind. He was brusque, but under all of his sharp thrusts there appeared the motive of kindness."[320]

In the last few months of his life, Goldrick, a distinguished-looking fellow, still attracted attention on the streets. The locals knew him, and newcomers quickly learned who he was. He became a quaint figure in the rapidly growing metropolis. During this time, when Denver was expanding and booming, the professor clung to his pioneer image. The slogan for his paper changed from "A Paper for the People" to "The Pioneer Paper of the New West." Though he was proud of the area's thriving success, it was apparent that he was more comfortable in the old West than in Denver's flashy newness.

People were fond of him, but he was no longer the center of powerful civic activities. One of his peers compared him to a piece of antique furniture that did not quite fit in the new parlor but was too valued to discard.[321] There were many well-dressed gentlemen on the streets of Denver in 1882. There also were many people who knew of Demosthenes and Prometheus. Though the professor could still catch the attention of a passerby, he no longer held the fascination of the more sophisticated citizens of Denver.

Only twenty-three years prior to Goldrick's death, the Apollo Hall was the place of entertainment in the mining camps. It was a large room above Libeus Barney's saloon, and the actors had to speak up strongly to be heard over the rowdy noise below. The hall, with its rough floors and hard wooden benches, was illuminated by candles. The townsfolk were delighted when the entertainment venue was upgraded to the somewhat improved People's Theater, and Goldrick was asked to give the opening poem.[322]

Two decades later, no one would have thought to ask the quirky professor to give an introductory poem at the Tabor Grand Opera House opening in 1881. The elaborately furnished building with 1,500 mohair seats could hold what had been the permanent population of Denver City and Auraria when Goldrick wowed and awed the pioneers in 1859. Just as he predicted that it would, his beloved town had become a thriving metropolis—it had outgrown him. His city fathers remembered him and no doubt delighted him when they placed a copy of his *Historical Sketch of Denver, Colorado* in the cornerstone of the new city hall, dedicated the year before his death.[323]

He left thousands of words produced by his sharp mind and his prodigious pen. Though many of those words are superfluous, they provide lively and vivid firsthand accounts of life in the West that gave Goldrick such a warm welcome and such a fond farewell. He can be remembered as a private man who put on his fine costume each day, strode out upon life's stage, and performed his role as the elegant, clever, eccentric Irishman with much to say. "His place in the drama of the city's history is that of the character artist. He filled the role to perfection."[324]

The best description of him was left to us by the newspaper that was quick to show confidence in his writing. The *Rocky Mountain News* described him thus:

> *His sharp features, piercing eyes, slight figure, always faultlessly dressed, his characteristic gait would attract attention in any crowd. The inquiry as to who he was was common, and the announcement that he was a genuine barnacle*[325] *was always received with surprise. The Professor never lost his native brogue entirely and its cling was just apparent enough to add a certain richness to his conversation, which was instructive, and for its short quick sentences, attractive.*[326]

During the twentieth century, feature articles about the professor appeared from time to time. University students occasionally wrote pieces about him. In 1927 he was portrayed in a pulp fiction novel, *Colorado,* by William MacLeod Raine. In the few pages in which he encounters the protagonist of the novel, the professor is shown in a positive light.[327]

In 1947 his Union School was commemorated by the Colorado Historical Society when the organization placed a bronze plaque on the side of a building where the school was believed to have been located.[328]

On This Site in Auraria (West Denver)
The First School in Colorado
Was Opened on October 3, 1859

"Professor" O. J. Goldrick, Who Came to Denver Dressed in
Frock Coat and Driving a Bull Team, Was the First Teacher.
The School House Was a Rented Log Cabin With Dirt Roof
and Canvas Door.
Pupils Paid $3.00 Per Month Tuition.
Free Public Schools Were Not Established Until 1862
Erected by the State Historical Society of Colorado from
The William S. Braiden Fund and by the American Pioneer
Trails Association and School Children of Denver. 1947.

The building on which the plaque was displayed has been razed. The site of Denver's first school is now appropriately part of the Auraria Higher Education Center campus.[329]

In 1950 Goldrick made *Time* magazine when Denver hosted a national group of educators. The article told of his entrance into Auraria in his fancy clothes, coaxing the oxen in Latin, and his establishment of the first school. The magazine's imaginative journalist reported that Goldrick's first words in Auraria were, "Set 'em up. The drinks are on me."[330]

In 1951 a group of students at Denver's Westwood School were commissioned to form an O. J. Goldrick Club; the purpose—to encourage and motivate young people with interest in becoming teachers.[331]

In recent years, Goldrick has been remembered less frequently in newspaper articles, possibly because so little new information about him has been available. Some modern histories of Denver and of Colorado do not mention him. However, he is not forgotten. When there is a school referendum or a pioneer celebration, the professor's story comes to life in feature articles. History professor Tom Noel managed to put a fresh spin on Goldrick's traditional story in a piece in the *Rocky Mountain News* in 2001 titled *Learning Came Early to Pioneers of Denver.*[332] After the 2013 Cherry Creek flood, Noel drew attention to Goldrick's masterful account of the flood of 1864. "He produced a first-hand flood account unmatched to this day despite valiant efforts to capture the horrors of last month's flooding by intrepid *Post* reporters."[333]

When he died, one of the professor's contemporaries wrote, "His death calls to mind many incidents in the life of this singular genius, which will someday creep into print and be handed down among the archives of Colorado, and will figure in the history of this glorious state many years hence."[334]

This biography is presented with as much truth as the currently available research material provides, and with the hope that the expansion of Goldrick's story may come with the discovery of more primary source material. As Professor Goldrick said, while posing as the Observer, "No 'sensation' items or one-sided accounts will ever be dispatched by me."[335]

Acknowledgments

Dr. Maury Haraway has supported my efforts from the beginning. In the early years of my research, Colorado historian Dr. Duane Smith provided encouragement and research tips. Gwenth Goldsberry was invaluable in the earlier research. Ray Hinchee of the Bayou Writers' Guild convinced me to complete the professor's story. My husband, James, was supportive throughout.

The library of the State Historical Society of Missouri provided digital copies of all thirty-four Observer articles written by Goldrick and published in the 1859 and 1860 *Missouri Democrat*. Stan Oliner, former curator for the Colorado Historical Society, encouraged my efforts by using my early donation of Goldrick documents to establish the Goldrick Family Collection. The Denver Public Library's Coi Drummond-Gehrig did an excellent job of locating and providing images. Sarah Gilmor of the Stephen H. Hart Library and Research Center, History Colorado Center was a consummate professional in finding answers among the archives of the library. I am indebted to Melissa VanOtterloo, Photo Research and Permissions Librarian for the Center, who helped me to understand the use of archived photographs and provided the photograph of the professor in his fancy duds for the book's cover. Keith Schrum, Senior Curator of Archives for the History Colorado Center, accepted the responsibility of preserving the full array of Goldrick documents I had acquired.

Goldrick family members provided oral history and precious family documents. Their willingness to share these documents made the biography possible. The contributors were great-great-nieces of the professor. Elizabeth (Betty) Rahel provided the story of her grandmother, Susan Goldrick Chapman Robinson, along with photographs. Ann Spichter allowed me to keep her great-great-grandfather's original diary for over a year so that I could compare it to the carefully typed transcription by Joan Marie Goldrick Johnson. Ms. Johnson provided valuable family information, along with a copy of her transcription of the diary. Frances Moody, Peggy Green, and Mary Clark met me in Denver and shared family history and letters. Mrs. Robert Perkins provided the contents of the shoe box found in her deceased husband's closet that contained Goldrick material from Lillian Goldrick Johnson. Each of these people provided pieces of the story. Bringing the parts together and forming the Goldrick Family Collection made the biography possible.

The professor has been whispering in my ear for thirty years. Errors in his story needed rectifying. During the process, he repaid my efforts. His writing sometimes made me laugh, and it enlightened me about life in the Centennial State in the mid-to late 1800s. While working on the professor's story, I acquired a renewed respect for the pioneer spirit that is woven into the fabric of our nation. Perhaps now that the biography is finished, I can rest, and our professor can rest in peace.

Margaret McLean Truly
margaretmtruly@gmail.com

Images

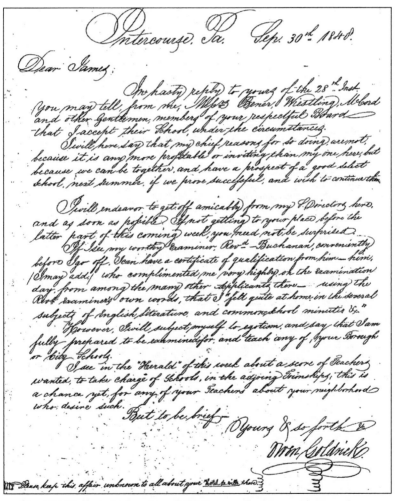

In this 1848 letter, Owen shows off his penmanship and boasts that he did well on the teacher certification examination and is ready to join James in Middletown, Pennsylvania, to teach. *Goldrick Family Collection, History Colorado Center, Denver, CO*

LITERARY NOTICE.

ENGLISH, MERCANTILE, MATHEMATICAL & CLASSICAL

SELECT SCHOOL,

MIDDLETOWN, PA.

J. & O. GOLDRICK,

RESPECTFULLY announce to the citizens of Middletown and vicinity that they are prepared to receive a select number of Pupils, (male and female,) to be correctly and thoroughly instructed in a course of sound education, suitable to prepare young Gentlemen for business or entrance into College; and to give young Ladies a thorough education in the branches of English Literature and the Sciences.

THE COURSE OF INSTRUCTION COMPRISES THE FOLLOWING STUDIES, VIZ:

Orthography,
Reading,
English Grammar & Composition,
Geography,
Arithmetic, theoretical and practical,
Book-Keeping,
Primary Drawing,
History, general and natural,
Geometry, Mensuration,

Philosophy, intellectual, moral and natural,
Chemistry, Botany & Physiology,
Algebra, elementary,
Trigonometry, plain & spherical,
Astronomy & the higher Mathematics, with the Latin and Greek Languages.

INSTRUCTION WILL BE GIVEN IN

PENMANSHIP,

Accomplishing young men in a permanent, current business hand, rapid in execution and alike adapted to all the useful purposes of life; and young ladies in a small, neat and elegant epistolary hand.

If desired, a class will be taught Land Surveying, reducing it to Field Practice, Mapping, &c.

☞By a prompt and judicious arrangement, combined with strict discipline in the management of their School, they trust to be able to secure the speedy improvement of the Pupils committed to their care.

☞**TERMS MODERATE.**

MIDDLETOWN, APRIL, 1848.

James Goldrick had this flyer printed to advertise a select school that he and Owen would conduct in the summer of 1848. *Goldrick Family Collection, History Colorado Center, Denver, CO*

Solutions.

QUESTION 2, BY A. FRESHMAN. Given the three angles of a triangle, 50°, 60°, 70° and the area 12 acres, to find the sides of the triangle.

SOLUTION. Let A, B,C, represent the required triangle, of which the angle A is 50°, B 60°, and C 70°. Denote the sines of the angles A, B, and C, by a, b, and c, and let AB$=x$:

Then as AB : AC :: sin C : sin B.

or x : AC :: c : b, hence AC $= \dfrac{bx}{c}$

Again, AB : BC :: sin C : sin A.

or x : BC :: c : a, hence BC $= \dfrac{ax}{c}$.

In the triangle CDB we have the proportion :
Rad : sin B :: BC : CD,

or $1 : b :: \dfrac{ax}{c} : \text{CD} = \dfrac{abx}{c}$.

But the area $= \dfrac{\text{CD} \times \text{AB}}{2c} = \dfrac{abx^2}{2c} = 120$ sq. chains.

hence $x = \sqrt{\dfrac{240c}{ab}} = 18.44 +$ chains.

$\dfrac{ax}{c} = 16.99 +$ chains, and $\dfrac{bx}{c} = 15.03$ chains.

ACKNOWLEDGMENTS. — Question 2 was solved by John J. Hooker, R. W. McFarland, D. Jamieson, and A. McLean. O. Goldricke furnished a solution to the question of C. A. Leeson, which came too late for notice in the March number.

James saved the May 1, 1850, issue of the *School Friend*, a teachers' journal in which Owen received recognition for submitting the correct answer to a mathematics challenge problem. *Goldrick Family Collection, History Colorado Center, Denver, CO*

Owen J. Goldrick during his early days in Denver. *Courtesy of Colorado State Archives and Denver Public Library, Western History Division, Call # F-181, Denver, CO*

This illustration of the McClure-Goldrick incident was published in A. D. Richardson's 1867 *Beyond the Mississippi*. It is evident that the illustrator had never seen the professor. Goldrick would not have worn rumpled clothing. His shoes would have been shiny patent leather, and his hat was always a top hat. At this period in his life, he had mutton-chop whiskers. *Courtesy of Denver Public Library, Western History Division, Call # C978.04 R395be. Denver, CO*

Professor Goldrick in 1866 during the time he was serving as coeditor of Salt Lake City's *DAILY UNION VEDETTE*. *Courtesy of Carte de Visite Collection, Scan # 10027713, History Colorado Center, Denver, CO*

**Professor Goldrick (right) standing beside the stairs to the second-floor
office of the** *Rocky Mountain Herald.* **The building was located in Denver's
Tappan Block on Fifteenth Street between Larimer and Holladay.
Goldrick lived in a comfortable hotel room in the block adjacent to the**
Herald **office.** *Courtesy of Denver Public Library, Western History Division, Call #
X-18527, Denver, CO*

> Under the head of "A Colorado Thoroughbred" the Boulder Voter talks in this style, which is to the point, and which we cordially endorse: "Prof. O. J. Goldrick, candidate for Superintendent of Public Instruction, is the acknowledged choice of *the people* for that position. He is a talented gentleman of refinement and ability, possessing all the necessary qualities requisite to hold the office. Being an old and experienced teacher he should receive the hearty support of *all*. He has the honor of having taught the first school and the first Sabbath school in Colorado. He was the founder of free schools in the New West, the first organizer of school districts in Denver and the first school superintendent ever elected in Arapahoe county; the first man who had the pluck to plant education in the heart of the "American desert," and thus timely aided in the first settlement and the first civilization of what is now the great Centennial State. In just recognation of the past labors, and as a 'Colorado thoroughbred,' Professor Goldrick deserves the generous suffrage of *all* political parties in all parts of this State which has so materially helped to shape, both as editor and educationist."

The August 28, 1878, *COLORADO TRANSCRIPT* called the professor a "Colorado Thoroughbred" in its endorsement of his candidacy for state superintendent of public instruction.

The June 7, 1879, front page of FRANK LESLIE'S ILLUSTRATED NEWSPAPER featured this illustration. The accompanying story did not mention Goldrick. It told about the first "swell" to visit Leadville. The subject of the sketch could have been the professor. In 1879 he was negotiating to bond his interest in a mine near Leadville. The depiction of the clothes, the cigar, and the strutting, confident stride are characteristic of the professor. The illustrator may not have seen the "swell" in person. If he had seen Goldrick, he would have drawn him with a beard. *Courtesy of Denver Public Library, Western History Division, Call # Z-87, Denver, CO*

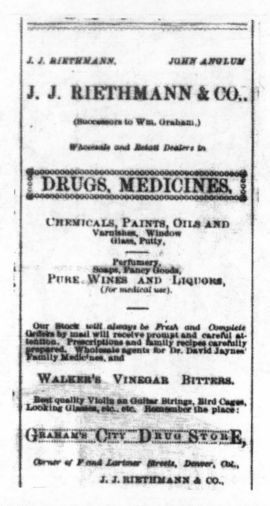

John J. Riethmann was a pioneer who settled in Colorado in 1858 and opened Denver's first drugstore the following year. He served as Goldrick's informal creditor, loaning him small sums from time to time. The professor always repaid the loans. Advertisements for Riethmann's drugstore were regular features in the ROCKY MOUNTAIN HERALD. *Rocky Mountain Herald, June 1, 1881*

Susan Goldrick Chapman Robinson was the professor's niece. Her father,
the stern Dr. William O. Goldrick, was infuriated when Susan eloped
at age nineteen, then later divorced her husband and returned home
with her young son and infant daughter, Lizzie. William felt that this was
an affront to the sanctity of marriage. He made her wear a lace cap to
cover her auburn hair and would not allow her to visit her friends. She
later had a happy marriage with Mr. Robinson, who gave her the onyx
earrings, gold chain, and jeweled broach. *Courtesy of Susan's granddaughter,
Elizabeth Rahel*

Professor Goldrick in the 1870s during the time of his marriage. *Courtesy of Denver Public Library, Western History Division, Call # F-381, Denver, CO*

A later photograph. *Courtesy Denver Public Library, Western History Division, Call # F-18899, Denver, CO*

William Goldrick wrote in his diary telling of the death of his brother Owen. *Courtesy of Virginia Ann Speicher, William's great-great-granddaughter. Copy in Goldrick Family Collection.*

The professor's great-great-great-nephew, Robert Johnson, is standing by the professor's headstone in Riverside Cemetery in Denver. Prior to his retirement, Johnson served as director of music programs for the Denver Public Schools and was organist for Saint Thomas Episcopal Church in Denver. *Author's collection.*

The author is shown in 1985 with the diary of Dr. William O. Goldrick. She was allowed to study the journal for over a year before returning it to the Goldrick family. Joan Marie Goldrick Johnson carefully transcribed the entire journal. *A copy of the transcript is in the Goldrick Family Collection, History Colorado Center, Denver, CO. Author's collection.*

The Owen J. Goldrick Elementary School on South Zuni Street in Denver was opened in September 1952. The cornerstone contains a brief biography of Goldrick, a copy of his *HISTORICAL SKETCH OF DENVER, COLORADO*, a copy of a book about the Denver Mint by Nolie Mumey and E. H. Gruber, several essays and a script from a play about early Colorado history written by Denver Public School students, and a miniature replica of Colorado's first school made in 1946 by Nancy West of Skinner Junior High School. *Courtesy of Subject File Collection, C-Denver Schools-Goldrick School, Scan # 10043628, History Colorado Center, Denver, CO*

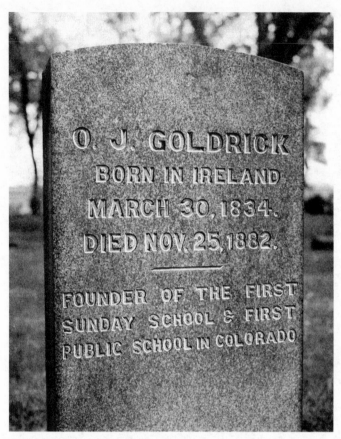

The professor's date of birth on his tombstone was probably taken from the minutes of the Colorado Pioneers. In those minutes, someone had written that his date of birth was March 30, 1836, then marked through that and changed the year to 1834. In a letter from his father the correct date is given as March 31, 1829. This was confirmed by his niece Susan in the family Bible. She recorded that her uncle's age at his death was 53 years, 7 months, and 25 days. The professor was thirty when he first arrived in Auraria with the wagon train. *Courtesy of Denver Public Library, Western History Division and Riverside Cemetery, Denver, CO*

Note from the Author

Why did I spend almost three decades seeking verifiable facts about Professor Goldrick? After all, I am not a citizen of Colorado. I'm a Louisiana native, now retired to Birmingham, Alabama. My family and I have spent as much time as possible in the Centennial State, hiking, climbing the fourteeners, trekking the Continental Divide, skiing, visiting parks, libraries, and museums, and reading the state's compelling history.

During the early '80s I was drawn to the quirky, brilliant Professor Goldrick. When I read what one of his journalist colleagues wrote in 1882—that no one knew enough about the professor to write his true history—the challenge was on. This led me to locate Goldrick's great-great-nieces. These were women in their sixties and seventies—gracious, generous, intelligent, and willing to share the family story and the precious family letters. Would you be willing to mail the highly personal diary of your great-great-grandfather to a stranger who lived hundreds of miles away? These descendants of the professor's older brother, William, wanted their great-great-uncle's story told fairly and accurately. The confidence they placed in me energized my effort.

A medical microbiologist by training, I had research skills in that field. I had to teach myself the art of researching historical documents, tracking references, locating and scanning reams of microfilm, and following every lead. My efforts included assuring that the documents entrusted to me were placed in the History Colorado Center—a safe repository for the documents placed in my care. Though there are gaps in the telling of it, the Goldrick story that the pundit said could never be written has been recorded. During this process I came to know Professor Goldrick and have enjoyed the pleasure of his company.

Endnotes

All diary entries, family letters, and documents noted are in the Goldrick Family Collection at the Stephen H. Hart Library and Research Center, History Colorado Center, Denver, Colorado.

Chapter 1

1. Oral history notes from six Goldrick family descendants. Many of the family letters to America were addressed from Sandfield. The family members state that efforts to locate birth and death records in Ireland were thwarted because these records belonged to the Catholic Church and were apparently destroyed when the family was excommunicated. In regard to Owen being spoiled, see Endnote # 4.

2. Letter from Owen Scott Goldrick, father of Owen Joseph Goldrick, to Senator Joseph Pollock in America, December 20, 1834. Pollock was a physician-farmer who lived near New Castle, Pennsylvania. He served for a time in the Pennsylvania legislature. It is not known how Goldrick knew him, but the two families were close. The Pollock family is mentioned several times in family letters.

3. Ibid. The father boasted to Senator Pollock that he had as good a farm as there was in Ireland.

4. In their letters and in William's diary the older brothers mention doing farm-work and manual labor. Evidence that Owen was not accustomed to manual labor is found in his letters to his brother James. When he first arrived in New York, he complained of chopping wood and hauling coal. As soon as he started earning pay as a teacher, he hired a boy to start his fire. Letter from Owen to James, November 7, 1847; undated letter from Owen to James from New York City; letter from Owen to James from Brownsville, Ohio, October 20, 1849. In later years, Goldrick's colleagues commented on his white hands that he protected with leather gloves.

5. Descendants of William Goldrick differ in their opinions as to which brother was the oldest. James listed his age as thirty-eight when he boarded ship to sail to America in 1847. He was probably born in 1809. William varies his age in his diary. In the 1880 census he gives his year of birth as "about 1811."

In an application for membership in the Sons of the American Revolution, he gives it as 1810. Conclusion: James is the oldest brother.

6. William Goldrick, older brother of Professor Goldrick, kept a diary. A precise transcription by William's great-great-granddaughter, Joan Marie Goldrick Johnson, is in the Goldrick Family Collection.

7. Ibid.

8. Diane Ravitch, *A Brief History of Teaching Professionalism*, www.ed.gov.

9. Diary entry, September 25, 1831.

10. Entries in William's diary indicate that after his family was excommunicated from the Catholic Church, he embraced a charismatic Protestant faith and was disappointed that his family was more conservative in their views. His brother James was a devout Episcopalian, and as a young man, Owen attended a Protestant Sunday school in Middletown, Pennsylvania. William's diary tells about his struggle with his faith, sometimes attending three churches in one day. James's religion is described in a letter of recommendation by W. Kenny to Bro. Ford, August 3, 1844; Knowledge of Owen's Sunday school affiliation comes from a letter to him from George Croles, August 21, 1850, telling how the church and Sunday school in Middletown, Pennsylvania, had grown since Owen moved.

11. Owen Scott Goldrick to Senator Pollock, December 20, 1834.

12. Silas W. Fowler, MD, *History of Medicine and Biographical Sketches of the Physicians of Delaware County* (published by author, 1910), Delaware County District Library, Delaware, Ohio. The article about Dr. William O. Goldrick contains an error. Matilda Halderman Goldrick is listed as his first wife, and Matilda is listed as his second wife. His second wife was Clarissa Halderman Goldrick, sister of his first wife.

13. Owen Scott Goldrick to Senator Pollock, December 20, 1834.

14. William's efforts to find a suitable wife, his marriage to Matilda, the birth of his children, and his dream of becoming a physician are described in his diary.

15. A frugal, compassionate, generous James Goldrick is described in William's diary and in the family letters.

16. One of the Goldrick descendants defended Patrick by stating that he was only sixteen when he arrived in America. No documentation is currently available to support this.

17. Owen Scott Goldrick to James and William. No date, but written shortly after Patrick emigrated in the fall of 1833.

18. Patrick to William, January 16, 1837. William forwarded the letter to James with a note included.

19. Diary entry, June 24, 1838.

20. Patrick to William, April 29, 1840. Letter forwarded from William to James.

21. Several of William's diary entries tell of his success selling maps and the difficulty of traveling so far from home. He wanted to study medicine and have a profession that would allow him to stay in one place and provide for his family.

22. Diary entry, November 8, 1842.

23. William to James, January 20, 1843.

24. Diary entry, April 28, 1844.

25. Diary entry, December 25, 1844; Letter from William to James, December 1, 1845.

26. Diary entry, December 10, 1848.

27. Diary entry, June 8, 1851. There are several other entries in which William chastises himself for being too critical of others.

28. Diary entry, March 14, 1847. In his diary, William refers to himself as a poor, ragged youth in Ireland. Poverty is relative. He may have felt poor compared to the family's circumstances before economic hardship hit Ireland. He or his father paid his passage to America. He was well educated enough to become a teacher shortly after his arrival.

Chapter 2

29. Ship roster, *Adario*. Sailed from Sligo, Ireland. Arrived in New York, NY, September 16, 1847. National Archives, Washington, DC. The roster states that Owen Goldrick was 17 ½ when he boarded ship. He was actually 18 ½. A letter from Owen's father to James, November 7, 1848, gives Owen's correct date of birth as March 31, 1829. This is further confirmed in a note written in a family memory Bible.

30. Owen to James, November 7, 1847.

31. Ibid.

32. Ibid. Apparently Owen believed that he was already capable of being a teacher.

33. Owen Scott Goldrick to James, May 25, 1848.

34. Undated letter from Owen to James, from same New York City address.

35. A copy of the original flyer is in the Goldrick Family Collection.

36. William to James and Owen, July 6, 1848.

37. Owen to James, September 30, 1848.

38. William to James, October 28, 1848.

39. Diary entry, October 22, 1848. James was frugal, thoughtful, and careful. The entry surely referred to Owen.

40. Owen Scott Goldrick to James, with comments directed to his son Owen Joseph, December 17, 1848.

41. Ibid.

42. Ibid.

43. James to his father and mother, March 6, 1850.

44. Owen to James, June 22, 1850. Owen relates in the letter that some Cornish malcontents who were jealous of his education tried to rough him up. The letter is overwritten in two directions to save postage and is difficult to read. A copy of the page from the *School Friend* saved by James is in the Goldrick Family Collection.

45. Diary entry, August 11, 1850; October 13, 1850, "Now I find myself alone, the latter with her dear babe, Josephine, lying in yonder grave yard and my other children 150 miles separated away from me." William was practicing medicine in Reynoldsburg, Ohio, and his wife's parents lived in Steubenville, Ohio. He and Matilda had an infant daughter named Hariett who was a toddler. She was allowed to be reared, and eventually adopted by the Hostetler family. This is not mentioned in the diary. The information came from Elizabeth Rahel, the great-granddaughter of Dr. Goldrick.

46. Owen Scott Goldrick to James, December 17, 1848; February 20, 1850.

47. Diary entry, February 23, 1851; Letter from James to his father and mother, March 6, 1850.

48. Diary entry, May 4 and 5, 1851.

49. Diary entries, October 3, October 31, 1852. William had a partnership with a Dr. Ewing that "will enable me to attend without a great deal of pecuniary loss, the College Course."

50. Diary entry, January 8, 1854. Married to Clarissa. "I am now the husband of my Clarissa. It is all pleasant and agreeable so far and I trust ever will be."

51. Owen to James, May 30, 1853.

52. Ibid.

53. Handwritten advertisement, Moore, Anderson and Company Publishers, written by Owen, saved by James, Goldrick Family Collection.

Chapter 3

54. Karen Mitchell, Doyle biographer, *History of the Doyle Family*, www.kmitch.com/Pueblo/index.html. Click on Resources, scroll to Family Pages, and click on Doyle Family and the Doyle Settlement.

55. *Rocky Mountain News*, January 1, 1873.

56. Numerous accounts describe Goldrick's attire, and few give the same descrip-

tion. Only one writer could be found who mentioned the embroidered vest; Joseph Emerson Smith, *The Colorado Magazine* 20:1 (1943): 7. Several accounts, including this one, state that Goldrick had the wagon train stop on the edge of town so that he could change into his fancy clothes.

57. The Fred mentioned in this piece is Fred Soloman, a business associate of Doyle's.

58. W. B. Vickers, *History of the City of Denver, Arapahoe County, and Colorado* (Chicago: O. L. Baskin and Company, 1880), 193.

59. A. J. Fynn and R. J. Hafen, *The Colorado Magazine* 12:1 (1935): 13–23.

60. *Rocky Mountain News*, August 22, 1859.

61. *Ibid.*, August 27, 1859.

Chapter 4

62. *The Denver Public Schools: The Story of Seventy-Five Years* published for the National Education Association meeting held in Denver, June 30–July 5, 1935, Denver Public School System archives.

63. O. J. Goldrick, *The Colorado Magazine* 6:2 (1929): 72–74.

64. Goldrick wrote an anonymous column for the *Missouri Democrat* signed "Observer." These letters from the *Pike's Peak Observer* were published in the *Democrat* from November 1859 until October, 1860. See bibliography.

65. *Rocky Mountain News*, November 17, 1859.

66. Ibid., January 4, 1860.

67. Ibid., February 1, 1860.

68. Arthur E. Pierce, *The Trail* 5:3 (1912): 5.

69. Levette H. Davidson, *The Colorado Magazine* 13:1 (1936): 30–31.

70. Goldrick writing as the Observer stated in several letters that all would not prosper, either as businessmen or miners, and that hard work and perseverance were needed. An example, *Missouri Democrat*, April 1, 1860.

71. Owen to James, December 15, 1859.

72. Owen to William, with advice for James. February 16, 1860.

73. Goldrick writing as the Observer, *Missouri Democrat*, February 1, 1860. Goldrick frequently used the word *spondulicks* when referring to money. He used it in letters to his brothers and in his writing in both the *Rocky Mountain News* and the *Missouri Democrat*.

74. Ibid.

75. Owen to William, February 16, 1860.

76. Henrietta E. Bromwell, *Fiftyniner's Directory* (Denver, for the Library of the City of Denver, 1926), 134.

77. Thomas to James, August 15, 1860.

78. George Croles, an old friend, to Owen telling him how Middletown, Pennsylvania, where Owen used to live, has grown, as has their church and the Sunday school they had attended. August 25, 1850.

79. Joseph Emerson Smith, *The Colorado Magazine* 20:1 (1943): 7–8.

80. Jerome C. Smiley, *History of Denver* (Denver: The Times-Sun Publishing Company, 1901): 764–765.

81. Arthur E. Pierce, *The Trail* 5:3 (1912): 5–7.

82. Goldrick writing as the Observer, *Missouri Democrat*, January 16, 1860; February 1, 1860.

83. Ibid., February 8, 1860.

84. Ibid., February 1, 1860.

85. Ibid., April 21, 1860.

86. Ibid., March 20, 1860.

87. Ibid., February 29, 1860; April 21, 1860.

88. Ibid., February 22, 1860. Goldrick frequently mentioned Demosthenes in his writing.

89. Letter of recommendation for James written by W. Kenny to Bro. Ford, August 3, 1844. States that James was a devout Episcopalian.

90. Goldrick writing as the Observer, February 8, 1860.

91. Ibid., January 9, 1860.

92. Ibid., March 22, 1860.

93. Ibid., May 12, 1860.

94. Ibid., April 18, 1860.

95. Albert D. Richardson, *Beyond the Mississippi* (Hartford: American Publishing Company, 1867), 186.

Chapter 5

96. Goldrick writing as the Observer, *Missouri Democrat*, January 16, 1860.

97. Ibid., February 8, 1860.

98. Ibid., December 10, 1859.

99. Ibid., April 18, 1860.

100. *Rocky Mountain News*, November 17, 1859. On the same date, Goldrick, writing as the Observer, used the same descriptive words that were printed in the *Missouri Democrat* on November 30, 1859.

101. Goldrick writing as the Observer altered the lines in the *Missouri Democrat*, April 21, 1860. He used the first four lines of the poem in the *Rocky Mountain News*, February 17, 1860, and used the altered line in the *News* on July 30, 1864.

102. Goldrick wrote three front-page articles from the mines signed "G" for the *Rocky Mountain News*, July 25, 1860; August 1, 1860; and August 22, 1860. During this time, the Observer skipped several weeks and then resumed his column, stating that he had been traveling in the mountains looking at the mines. *Missouri Democrat*, September 1, 1860.

103. Goldrick writing as the Observer wrote complimentary comments about Whitsitt. *Missouri Democrat*, January 16, 1860; February 8, 1860. Accounts of the McClure-Goldrick incident; J. E. Wharton, *History of Denver* (Denver: D. O. Wilhelm, 1866), 43–48. Albert D. Richardson, *Beyond the Mississippi* (Hartford: American Publishing Company, 1867), 305–306.

104. Goldrick writing as the Observer, *Missouri Democrat*, February 15, 1860.

105. Ibid., February 22, 1860.

106. *Philadelphia Inquirer*, November 26, 1860. Written by a correspondent for the *New York Tribune*. The journalist uses some of the same phrases that A. D. Richardson used in his account of this incident in *Beyond the Mississippi*. In this article, the initials for McClure should be W. P. and the initials for Goldrick should be O. J.

107. *Rocky Mountain Herald*, October 18, 1860.

108. *Rocky Mountain News*, October 30, 1860.

109. Ibid.

110. Ibid., November 7, 1860.

111. Ibid., November 3, 1860.

112. The citizens siding with the local government was a positive event for Denver and for Goldrick.

113. Goldrick writing as the Observer, *Missouri Democrat*, September 1, 1860.

114. H. R. Vendemoer, *The Denver Monthly Western Roundup* 14:12 (1958): 9–10.

Chapter 6

115. *Omaha World*, December 15, 1860, reprinted in *Omaha World Herald*, December 15, 1960.

116. Thomas F. Dawson, *The Colorado Magazine*, 6:4 (1929).

117. *Denver Public Schools*, published for the National Education Association

meeting in Denver, June 30–July 5, 1935. Archives, Denver Public Schools.

118. *Rocky Mountain News*. December 2, 1861.

119. A. J. Fynn and L. R. Hafen, *The Colorado Magazine* 12:1 (1935): 13–23.

120. Jerome C. Smiley, *History of Denver* (Denver: *The Denver Times*, 1901): 732.

121. Levette Jay Davidson, *The Colorado Magazine* 13:1 (1936): 26–37.

122. Marshall Sprague, *Colorado: A Bicentennial History* (New York: W. W. Norton, 1976), 34–35.

123. Notes on oral history from William's descendants, Goldrick Family Collection.

124. Diary entry, December 5, 1841. Charles Ball's narrative was published in 1837. It was republished by Dover Publications in 1990 and again in 2003 using the title *Fifty Years in Chains*. The young William's Civil War record, *History of Union County, Ohio* (Chicago: W. H. Beers and Company, 1883), 492.

125. Levette Jay Davidson, *The Colorado Magazine* 13:1 (1936): 13–23. Goldrick's canvassing trip and letters to the *Rocky Mountain News* began on December 2, 1863, and continued in a series through April 6, 1864.

126. *Denver Tribune*, November 22, 1882.

127. Robert L. Perkins, *The First Hundred Years: An Informal History of Denver and the Rocky Mountain News* (New York: Doubleday and Company Inc., 1959), 220.

128. Thomas to William, September 4, 1864.

129. Ibid.

130. Thomas to James, October 15, 1864.

131. W. B. Bateham to James, November 29, 1864.

132. Levette J. Davidson, *The Colorado Magazine* 13:1 (1936): 30.

133. *Rocky Mountain News*, May 18, 1865.

Chapter 7

134. J. Cecil Alter, *Early Journalism* (Salt Lake City: Utah State Historical Society, 1938), 361–375. Source of information in this chapter about the *Union Vedette* and Goldrick's time at this paper.

135. Ibid.

136. Owen Scott Goldrick to James, with words directed to Owen Joseph, December 17, 1848.

137. *Rocky Mountain News*, November 1, 1866.

138. *Denver Tribune*, November 27, 1882.

139. Levette J. Davidson, *The Colorado Magazine* 13:1 (1936): 26–37.

140. Letter from Thomas to James, June 1, 1867.

141. *Rocky Mountain News*, May 3, 1867.

142. Douglas C. McMurtrie and Albert H. Allen, *Early Printing in Colorado* (Denver: Carnegie Regional Grant, A. B. Hirschfeld Press, 1935), 49–50.

Chapter 8

143. *Rocky Mountain News*, October 2, 1867.

144. Ibid., October 15, 1867.

145. William N. Byers, *Encyclopedia of Biography of Colorado, History of Colorado* (Chicago: Century Publishing and Engraving Company, 1901), 40.

146. *Springfield Republican*, March 20, 1869.

147. *Rocky Mountain News*, September 5, 1867.

148. Ibid., July 24, 1868, in an advertisement placed by Goldrick in the *News*.

149. Thomas to James, May 3, 1869.

150. Douglas C. McMurtrie and Albert H. Allen, *Early Printing in Colorado* (Denver: A. B. Hirschfeld Press, 1935), 49–50.

151. *Rocky Mountain News*, September 9, 1870.

152. Ibid., January 1871. Goldrick is traveling with another journalist who tells the story.

153. Ibid., October 27 and 28, 1871.

154. Ibid., February 4, 1872.

155. *Rocky Mountain Herald*, February 10, 1872.

156. William to James. James is at Sandfield. November 2, 1871.

157. *Rocky Mountain Herald*, March 27, 1875.

158. Ibid., January 1, 1881.

159. Diary entry December 28, 1873.

160. *Rocky Mountain Herald*, July 15, 1876.

161. *Denver Republican*, September 13, 1883.

162. *Rocky Mountain News*, January 26, 1881.

163. *Rocky Mountain Herald*, June 22, 1876.

164. Ibid., March 7, 1868.

165. Ibid., September 9, 1876.

166. Ibid., May 11, 1872.

167. Ibid., April 15, 1876.

168. W. B. Vickers, *History of Denver the City of, Arapahoe County, and the State of Colorado* (Chicago: O. L. Baskin and Company, 1880), 451.

169. *Rocky Mountain News*, November 26, 1882.

170. *Rocky Mountain Herald*, October 31, 1874.

171. Ibid., March 27, 1875.

172. Melvin Schoberlin, *From Candles to Footlights* (Denver: Old West Publishing Company, 1941), 200, 207.

173. *Rocky Mountain Herald*, May 9, 1869.

174. Ibid., September 23, 1876.

175. Ibid., February 10, 1872.

176. Ibid., October 16, 1875; September 16, 1876.

177. Ibid., August 26, 1876.

178. Ibid., July 15, 1871.

179. Ibid., April 25, 1868.

180. Ibid., October 28, 1876.

Chapter 9

181. *Santa Fe Daily News*, Monday, May 12, 1873.

182. *Rocky Mountain News*, May 7, 1873.

183. *Rocky Mountain Herald*, November 17, 1877. Most of what is known about Edith and her illness is in this tribute written by her husband.

184. Minutes of the Association of Colorado Pioneers, April 29, 1876, Denver Public Library. In the newspapers of this era the organization bore this name. In later years it has been called the Society of Colorado Pioneers.

185. *Rocky Mountain News*, August 1, 1976.

186. *The Colorado Magazine* 3:3 (1926): 94–97.

187. Goldrick published his historical sketch on a handbill and distributed copies to his *Herald* readers. A copy of the speech was reproduced in Nolie Mumey's Goldrick biography, *Professor Oscar J. Goldrick and His Denver* (1959).

188. *Rocky Mountain News*, August 1, 1906.

189. Ibid., July 30, 1876.

190. *Rocky Mountain Herald*, November 17, 1877.

191. Diary entry, October 22, 1876.

192. Lillian Goldrick Johnson (the professor's great-niece) to Robert Perkins, March 15, 1958. Goldrick Family Collection.

193. *Denver Times*, November 16, 1877.

194. *Rocky Mountain Herald*, November 17, 1877.

195. Diary entry, January 6, 1878.

196. Diary entry, December 26, 1878.

197. R. G. Dill, *The Political Campaigns of Colorado* (Denver: Arapahoe Publishing Company, 1895), 5–46.

198. W. B. Vickers, *History of Denver the City of, Arapahoe County, and Colorado* (Chicago: O. L. Baskin and Company, 1880), 451.

199. *Rocky Mountain News*, November 26, 1882.

200. Ibid., August 19, 1879.

201. The Colorado School of Mines Digital Collection cites *Engineering and Mining Journal* 28(9): 148–49.

202. Goldrick estate papers, 1882–1886, Colorado State Archives.

203. *Rocky Mountain News*, November 22, 1881.

204. *Rocky Mountain News*, January 1, 1873.

205. *Denver Times*, November 27, 1882.

206. Goldrick's obituaries mentioned that, toward the end of his life, he drifted away from his pioneer friends' more conventional path.

207. Owen Scott Goldrick to James, with comments directed to Owen Joseph, December 18, 1848.

208. See chapter 11.

209. Diary entry, December 31, 1882.

210. Silas W. Fowler, MD, *History of Medicine and Biographical Sketches of the Physicians of Delaware County* (Published by author, 1910) Delaware County District Library, Delaware, Ohio.

211. The author met Robert Johnson in Denver while doing research. Matthew Goldrick has a web page that describes his work in linguistics.

212. Letter from Betty Rahel to the author, with a note attached telling the places where James taught or served as principal. March 7, 1983.

Chapter 10

213. Bill Barker and Jackie Lewin, *Denver!* (Garden City, New York: Doubleday and Company Inc., 1972), 179.

214. Frank Hall, *History of the State of Colorado, Volume III* (Chicago: Blakely Printing Company, 1891), 135.

215. Frank Hall, *Denver Post*, April 18, 1903.

216. Janet Lecompte, *Journal of the Southwest* 38:1 (1996): 81–94. Lecompte presented this paper at the Colorado Historical Society in 1987 and subsequently published it in 1996.

217. *Rocky Mountain News*, April 12, 1864. The *News* reprinted an article about Goldrick's writing that had appeared in the *New York Courier*, in which the author teasingly referred to Goldrick's writing as the "Himalaya of Style," and then quoted an excerpt from one of the professor's travel pieces.

218. The letters from this canvassing trip to the *Rocky Mountain News* began being published on December 3, 1863, and continued in a series through April 6, 1864.

219. *Rocky Mountain News*, November 26, 1882.

220. Robert L. Perkins, *The First Hundred Years: An Informal History of Denver and the Rocky Mountain News* (New York: Doubleday and Company Inc., 1959), 212. Perkins did not have access to William's diary. From one of the family letters, he assumed (p.148) that Owen may have come to America at age "five or younger." That letter was actually referring to older brother Patrick. The diary tells us that Owen first came to America at age eighteen. Also, Perkins wrote that Patrick fought in the Civil War. Patrick joined the army during the Mexican-American War and was never heard from again. On page 149 of his book, Perkins wrote that Goldrick "also served as superintendent of schools for Boulder County from 1871–73." Perkins does not footnote this information, and no proof can be found to support it. According to the State Publications Library for Colorado (spl@cde.state.co.us), "the superintendent of Boulder County Schools in 1870–71 was A. R. Day, then Charles E. Sherman served 1872–1875."

221. en.wikipedia.org/wiki/LeRoy Hafen.

222. LeRoy R. Hafen and Ann W. Hafen, eds., *Reports from Colorado: The Wildman Letters, 1859–1865 with Other Related Letters and Newspaper Reports, 1859*, vol. 13, Southwest Historical Series (Glendale, CA: Arthur H. Clark Co., 1961), 1–20.

223. Ibid., 90.

224. Note that the Observer letters were dated several days before they were published. We use the publication date in our reference note.

225. Goldrick writing as the Observer, *Missouri Democrat*, November 22, 1859.

226. LeRoy R. Hafen and Ann W. Hafen, eds., *Reports from Colorado*, 212.

227. See the bibliography for more detailed information about Goldrick's Observer letters to the *Missouri Democrat*.

228. LeRoy R. Hafen and Ann W. Hafen, *Reports from Colorado*, 229.

229. Robert G. Athearn, *The Coloradans* (Albuquerque: University of New Mexico Press, 1976). Chapter 3, page 37; Chapter 4, page 50, "Another miner praised both Fisher and Jacob Adriance, both of whom he said had made greater sacrifices than 'half a dozen of your advertised D.D.s in their cushioned pulpits and stained glass windows of the East!'" These words did not come from a miner. They came from Goldrick writing as the Observer, *Missouri Democrat*, December 10, 1859. Athearn footnoted this as November 24, 1859. That was the date the letter was written. It was published on December 10; chapter 10, page 174, "'His train of flour, corn, seed wheat, barley, potatoes, etc., will arrive in a few days,' one of the miners reported." This report was not from a miner, but from Goldrick writing as the Observer, *Missouri Democrat*, November 30, 1859.

230. Goldrick writing as the Observer, *Missouri Democrat*, December 28, 1859.

231. *Rocky Mountain Herald*, October 16, 1875.

Chapter 11

232. Diary entry, September 23, 1849. James and Owen were visiting William and his family. William wrote, "We are a queer family, singular, and peculiar." James was the stable, helpful, frugal brother. It is doubtful that he was the subject of this comment. In his lifetime, Owen garnered such comments from many people.

233. W. B. Vickers, *History of the City of Denver, Arapahoe County, and Colorado* (Chicago: O. L. Baskin and Company, 1880), 451; *Silver World*, December 2, 1882.

234. *Colorado Gambler*, August 10, 2010.

235. "He said he was a graduate of Trinity College, Dublin . . . ," *Rocky Mountain News*, May 19, 1946; "Goldrick proclaimed that he was a graduate of Trinity College, Dublin, Columbia University, and a scholar . . . ," *The Rocky Mountain Herald Reader* (New York: William Morrow and Company, 1966).

236. Jerome C. Smiley, *History of Denver* (Denver: Times-Sun Publishing Company, 1901), 732.

237. Vickers, *History of the City of Denver*, 451.

238. *Denver Republican*, November 13, 1883; *Silver World*, December 2, 1882.

239. Vickers, *History of the City of Denver*. On page 451, "Professor Goldrick is a forcible, trenchant writer, is fearless and outspoken in manner, has little regard for the conventionalities of society, and heartily detests shame and hypocrisy in all its forms." In an obituary article in the *Denver Tribune*, No-

vember 26, 1882, the sentence was repeated in past tense. "Prof. Goldrick was a forcible, trenchant writer, fearless and outspoken in his manner, had little regard for the conventionalities of society and heartily detested sham and hypocrisy in all its forms." Did Vickers write this obituary, or did someone lift his sentence from his book?

240. *Silver World*, December 2, 1882.

241. *Rocky Mountain News*, December 5, 1882.

242. Harry Hansen, ed., *Colorado: A Guide to the Highest State* (New York: Hastings House, 1941, revised edition, 1970), 38.

243. *Denver Post*, April 18, 1903.

244. Nolie Mumey, *Professor Oscar J. Goldrick and His Denver* (Denver: Sage Books, 1959), 9. The master of arts degree was reported as early as 1927. Authors Henderson, Renaud, Goodykoontz, Barrett, and Mckeehan, *Colorado Short Studies of the Past and Present* (Boulder: University of Colorado, 1927), 123. Harry M. Barrett, one of the authors, revealed in a paper in 1935 that the college degrees did not exist. See Endnote # 245.

245. Harry M. Barrett, University of Colorado Bulletin 35:11 (April 11, 1935): 38.

246. Robert L. Perkins, *The First Hundred Years: An Informal History of Denver and the Rocky Mountain News* (New York: Doubleday and Company Inc., 1959), 147. In 1964 Joan Marie Goldrick Johnson wrote to Trinity College in Dublin and to Columbia University, and both denied any record of Goldrick having attended. The author checked both schools again and got the same reply.

247. Original flyer published by James Goldrick, Middletown, Pennsylvania, 1848, Goldrick Family Collection.

248. *Rocky Mountain News*, September 29, 1859.

249. Ibid., October 20, 1859.

250. *Rocky Mountain Herald*, August 2, 1876.

251. *Colorado Transcript*, August 28, 1878.

252. There were three younger brothers to choose from. William and Patrick were in America. John, Thomas, and Owen were still at home in Ireland.

253. *Rocky Mountain News*, January 25, 1860.

254. *Denver Tribune*, November 27, 1882.

255. Examples: Perkins, *The First Hundred Years*, 152; *Rocky Mountain Herald*, April 30, 1966; *Rocky Mountain News*, November 7, 1967.

256. S. T. Sopris, *The Trail* 7:2 (1914): 11.

257. Levette J. Davidson, *The Colorado Magazine* 13:1 (1936): 28–29.

258. *Silver World*, December 2, 1882.

259. Levette J. Davidson, *The Colorado Magazine* 13:1 (1936): 30–31.

260. *Rocky Mountain News*, June 11, 1866.

261. *Colorado Transcript*, January 16, 1867.

262. In his February 22, 1868, issue of the *Herald*, Goldrick listed several newspapers that had written favorable notices about his paper.

263. Reprinted in the *Rocky Mountain Herald*, February 22, 1868.

264. *Denver Republican*, September 13, 1883.

265. S. T. Sopris, *The Trail* 7:2 (1914): 5–11.

266. Stanley H. Zamonski and Teddy Keller, *The 59ers* (Frederick, CO: Platte'n Press, 1983), 63.

267. *Rocky Mountain News*, May 19, 1946.

268. *Denver Times*, November 28, 1882.

269. *Denver Tribune*, November 27, 1882.

270. *Rocky Mountain Herald*, November 17, 1877.

271. Obituaries state that Goldrick died in his room at the Condon House in the Tappan Block, corner of Fifteenth and Holladay. Though there is no Condon house listed in the city directories for 1881–82, there is a Carleton House owned by Mr. Condon located on Holladay between Fourteenth and Fifteenth. Goldrick's friends may have called this hotel the Condon House colloquially because it was owned by Mr. Condon. Goldrick's *Herald* office was also in the Tappan Block between Larimer and Holladay. This would mean that he lived within an easy walk to his office. The houses of prostitution were located on Holladay several blocks away. *Denver Tribune*, November 26, 1882; *Rocky Mountain News*, November 26, 1882; Clark Secrest, *Hell's Belles* (Boulder: University Press of Colorado, revised edition, 2002), 105.

272. O. J. Goldrick estate records, 1882–1886, Colorado State Archives. Hitchcock lamps had a wind-up fan incorporated in the base to prevent overheating and smoking.

273. *Denver Tribune*, November 26, 1882.

274. *Denver Republican*, September 13, 1883.

275. *Denver Tribune*, November 27, 1882. Goldrick's friends assumed he was Catholic because he was Irish. Apparently they knew nothing about his background and his family's excommunication from the church. Bishop Machebeuf, a Catholic priest, was sent away by Goldrick, who then asked to give his final confessions to a Protestant minister, Dr. Jeffreys.

276. *Denver Tribune*, November 27, 1882.

277. John J. Riethmann interviewed by T. F. Dawson. In early lists of pioneers, Riethmann's name is spelled with an "ei" rather than "ie." In the ads in the

Rocky Mountain News, the name is spelled "Riethmann."

278. *Rocky Mountain News*, November 26, 1882.

279. *Denver Times*, November 28, 1882.

280. Documentation provided by Denver Press Club Historian Alan J. Kania. Copy placed in Goldrick Family Collection.

281. *Denver Times*, November 28, 1882.

282. *Rocky Mountain News*, November 28, 1882.

283. *Denver Times*, November 27, 1882.

284. *Springfield Republican*, July 19, 1879.

285. Owen Goldrick to his great-niece Lizzie, November 17, 1882.

286. Notes of oral history from collateral descendants and a conversation between the author and Betty Rahel, Goldrick Family Collection. Betty, Susan's granddaughter, described how Susan's divorce was viewed by her father.

287. Ibid.

288. John J. Riethmann, interviewed by T. F. Dawson.

289. *Denver Tribune*, November 27, 1882.

290. *Silver World*, December 2, 1882.

291. *Denver Times*, November 28, 1882.

292. Ibid.

293. *Denver Tribune*, November 27, 1882.

294. Ibid., November 28, 1882.

295. Owen Goldrick estate papers, 1882–1886, Colorado State Archives.

296. *Rocky Mountain News*, August 19, 1879. "A reporter of the *News* was shown a private letter from Leadville last night stating that parties offered to bond a mine in which Prof. Goldrick is interested for $20,000 for ninety days. The property is near the iron mine and is scarcely developed. The offer to bond comes from Chicago parties. The *News* congratulates Prof. Goldrick on his good luck and says, 'Good on your old head, Goldrick!' on his refusal to bond." Also see chapter 9, Endnote #196 that tells of Goldrick bonding a mine near Leadville.

297. *Rocky Mountain News*, November 26, 1882.

298. Owen Goldrick estate papers, 1882–86, Colorado State Archives.

299. John J. Riethmann interviewed by T. F. Dawson.

300. Owen Scott Goldrick to his son James with comments directed to young Owen, December 17, 1848.

301. Owen Goldrick estate papers, 1882–86, Colorado State Archives.

302. Levette J. Davidson, *The Colorado Magazine* 13:1 (1936): 37.

303. Vickers, *History of the City of Denver*, 192.

304. *Rocky Mountain Herald*, November 4, 1972. The Thomas Hornsby Ferrils sold the paper to Cle Cervi Symons in August of 1972.

305. Owen Goldrick estate papers, 1882–86, Colorado State Archives.

306. *Rocky Mountain Herald*, November 4, 1972.

307. Francis M. Bain to the author, February 22, 1984. In the Goldrick Family Collection.

308. Goldrick was elected to the position at the end of 1861 and served a two-year term, 1862 and 1863.

309. Information about the school's dedication was provided by the Denver Public School System from their archives.

Chapter 12

310. *Colorado Springs Weekly Gazette*, January 15, 1881.

311. Minutes of Association of Colorado Pioneers, 1881, Denver Public Library.

312. Alan J. Kania, Historian, Denver Press Club, *Denver Press Club History*, www.denverpressclub.org.

313. *Denver Tribune*, November 26, 1882.

314. *Rocky Mountain News*, June 9, 1882.

315. Ibid., January 26, 1881.

316. *Rocky Mountain Herald*, June 26, 1875.

317. O. J. Goldrick, *The Colorado Magazine* 6:2 (1929): 72–74.

318. *Denver Times*, November 27, 1882.

319. Ibid.

320. *Rocky Mountain News*, November 26, 1882.

321. *Denver Tribune*, November 26, 1882.

322. See chapter 6.

323. Nolie Mumey, *Professor Oscar J. Goldrick and His Denver* (Denver: Sage Books, 1959). When the city hall was razed years later, the history was found in the cornerstone.

324. *Denver Tribune*, November 27, 1882.

325. Pioneers from 1858 and 1859 were referred to as "barnacles."

326. *Rocky Mountain News*, November 26, 1882.

327. William MacLeod Raine, *Colorado* (New York: Grosset and Dunlap, 1927).

328. *Denver Post*, April 27, 1947; Agnes Wright Spring, *Denver's Historic Markers, Memorials, Statues, and Parks* (Denver: State Historical Society of Colorado, State Museum, 1959).

329. Thomas J. Noel, *Rocky Mountain News*, August 18, 2001.

330. *Time*, February 20, 1950.

331. *Rocky Mountain News*, February 5, 1951.

332. Ibid., August 18, 2001.

333. Thomas J. Noel, www.DenverPost.com, posted October 11, 2013; updated October 14, 2013.

334. *Denver Tribune*, November 27, 1882.

335. Goldrick writing as the Observer, *Missouri Democrat*, November 22, 1859.

Bibliography

Letters, Diary, Documents

Primary source material in the Goldrick Family Collection, Stephen H. Hart Library and Research Center, History Colorado Center, Denver, Colorado.

Books

1. Alter, Cecil. *Early Utah Journalism*. Salt Lake City, 1938.

2. Athearn, Robert G. *The Coloradans*. Albuquerque, 1976.

3. Ball, Charles. *Fifty Years in Chains*. Mineola, 2003. Originally published in 1837.

4. Barker, Bill and Jackie Lewin. *Denver!* Garden City, 1972.

5. Bromwell, Henrietta E. *Fiftyniner's Directory: Colorado Argonauts, 1858–59*. Denver, 1926.

6. Byers, William N. *Encyclopedia of Biography of Colorado*. Chicago, 1901.

7. Dill, R. G. *The Political Campaigns of Colorado*. Denver, 1895.

8. Fowler, Silas W., *History of Medicine and Biographical Sketches of the Physicians of Delaware County*. Delaware, 1910.

9. Hafen, LeRoy R. and Ann W. Hafen, eds. *Reports from Colorado: The Wildman Letters, 1859–65, with Other Related Letters and Newspaper Reports, 1859*, Vol. 13, Southwest Historical Series. Glendale, 1961.

10. Halaas, David F. *Boom Town Newspapers*. Albuquerque, 1981.

11. Hall, Frank. *History of the State of Colorado*, Vol. III. Chicago, 1891.

12. Hansen, Harry. *Colorado: A Guide to the Highest State*. New York, 1970.

13. Henderson, Renaud, Goodykoontz, Barrett, and Mckeehan. *Colorado Short Studies*. Boulder, 1927.

14. *History of Union County, Ohio*, Vol. 1, Chicago, 1883.

15. McMurtrie, Douglas C., and Albert H. Allen. *Early Printing in Colorado*. Denver, 1935.

16. Mumey, Nolie. *Professor Oscar J. Goldrick and His Denver*. Denver, 1959.

17. Perkins, Robert L. *The First Hundred Years: An Informal History of Denver and the Rocky Mountain News*. New York, 1959.

18. Raine, William MacLeod. *Colorado*. New York, 1927.

19. Richardson, Albert D. *Beyond the Mississippi*. Hartford, 1867.

20. Schoberlin, Melvin. *From Candles to Footlights*. Denver, 1941.

21. Secrest, Clark. *Hell's Belles*. Boulder, 2002.

22. Smiley, Jerome C. *History of Denver*. Denver, 1901.

23. Sprague, Marshall. *Colorado: A Bicentennial History*. New York, 1976.

24. Spring, Agnes Wright. *Denver's Historic Markers, Memorials, Statues, and Parks*. Denver, 1959.

25. Vickers, W. H. *History of the City of Denver, Arapahoe County, and Colorado*. Chicago, 1880.

26. Wharton, J. E. *History of Denver*. Denver, 1866.

27. Zamonski, Stanley W. and Teddy Keller. *The 59ers*. Frederick, 1983.

Journals, Magazines

1. Association of Colorado Pioneers (later called Society of Colorado Pioneers), Minutes of Meetings, Denver Public Library.

2. *Denver Monthly Western Roundup* 14:12 (1958).

3. *Engineering and Mining Journal* 28:9, 148–49. See digital collection, Colorado School of Mines.

4. *Journal of the Southwest* 38:1(1996).

5. *The Colorado Magazine* 3:3 (1926); 6:2 (1929); 6:4 (1929); 12:1 (1935); 13:1 (1936); 20:1 (1943).

6. *The Trail* 5:3 (1912); 7:2 (1914).

7. *Time*, February 20, 1950.

8. *University of Colorado Bulletin*, 35:11 (1935).

Newspapers

Colorado Springs Weekly Gazette, Colorado Transcript, Denver Post, Denver Republican, Denver Times, Denver Tribune, Missouri Democrat, New York Courier, Omaha World, Philadelphia Inquirer, Rocky Mountain Herald, Rocky Mountain News, Santa Fe Daily News, Silver World, Springfield Republican, Union Vedette.

Goldrick's letters as the Observer were printed in the *Missouri Democrat* on the following dates: November 22, 1859; November 30, 1859; December 10, 1859; December 12, 1859; December 20, 1859; December 28, 1859; January 9, 1860; January 16, 1860; January 24, 1860; February 1, 1860; February 8, 1860; February 15, 1860; February 22, 1860; February 29, 1860; March 13, 1860; March 20, 1860; March 22, 1860; March 28, 1860; April 4, 1860; April 11, 1860; April 18, 1860; April 21, 1860; April 30, 1860; May 5, 1860; May 12, 1860; June 11, 1860; June 16, 1860; June 23, 1860; July 20, 1860; September 1, 1860; September 10, 1860; September 15, 1860; September 24, 1860; October 11, 1860. The letter published on May 5, 1860, is the only letter in the series that did not include the word "Observer" at the end. The letters are dated, however, in our notes and references. The dates they were published are the dates used. Digital copies of the *Missouri Democrat* are available at the library of the Historical Society of Missouri.

Internet

DenverPost.com

coloradohistoricnewspapers.org

denverpressclub.org

ed.gov

en.wikipedia.org/wiki/LeRoy_Hafen

kmitchell.com/Pueblo/index.html

spl@cde.state.CO.US

Archives

Colorado State Archives

Denver Public School System Archives

Denver Press Club Archives, Alan J. Kania, Historian

Goldrick Family Collection, Stephen H. Hart Library and Research Center, History Colorado

Manuscripts

John J. Riethmann interviewed by T. F. Dawson, March 29, 1922. Subject files, Goldrick, Owen J., Stephen H. Hart Library and Research Center, History Colorado Center, Denver, CO.

Index